PENGUIN BOOKS
Getting to Know the General

Graham Greene was born in 1904 and educated at Berkhamsted School, where his father was headmaster. On coming down from Balliol College, Oxford, where he published a book of verse, he worked for four years as a sub-editor on *The Times*. He established his reputation with his fourth novel, *Stamboul Train*, which he classed as an 'entertainment' in order to distinguish it from more serious work. In 1935 he made a journey across Liberia, described in *Journey Without Maps*, and on his return was appointed film critic of the *Spectator*. In 1926 he had been received into the Roman Catholic Church and was commissioned to visit Mexico in 1938 and report on the religious persecution there. As a result he wrote *The Lawless Roads* and, later, *The Power and the Glory*.

Brighton Rock was published in 1938 and in 1940 he became literary editor of the *Spectator*. The next year he undertook work for the Foreign Office and was sent out to Sierra Leone in 1941–3. One of his major post-war novels, *The Heart of the Matter*, is set in West Africa and is considered by many to be his finest book. This was followed by *The End of the Affair*, *The Quiet American*, a story set in Vietnam, *Our Man in Havana* and *A Burnt-Out Case*. Many of his novels and short stories have been filmed, and *The Third Man* was written as a film treatment. His other publications include *The Pleasure Dome* (1972), *The Honorary Consul* (1973), *An Impossible Woman: The Memories of Dottoressa Moor of Capri* (edited 1975), *The Human Factor*, *Doctor Fischer of Geneva or The Bomb Party* (1980), *Monsignor Quixote* (1982) and *J'Accuse: The Dark Side of Nice* (1982). His first volume of autobiography was *A Sort of Life* (1971), and *Ways of Escape*, a second autobiographical volume, was published in 1980.

In all, Graham Greene has w͏ ͏⋯ ͏ ͏ ͏
which have been publishe͏
plays, children's books, trav͏
and short stories. He was ma͏

GRAHAM GREENE

GETTING TO KNOW THE GENERAL

The Story of an Involvement

I go, but I return: I would I were
The pilot of the darkness and the dream

– Alfred, Lord Tennyson

Penguin Books

Penguin Books Ltd, Harmondsworth, Middlesex, England
Viking Penguin Inc., 40 West 23rd Street, New York, New York 10010, U.S.A.
Penguin Books Australia Ltd, Ringwood, Victoria, Australia
Penguin Books Canada Ltd, 2801 John Street, Markham, Ontario, Canada L3R 1B4
Penguin Books (N.Z.) Ltd, 182–190 Wairau Road, Auckland 10, New Zealand

First published by The Bodley Head Ltd 1984
Published in Penguin Books 1985

Made and printed in Great Britain by
Cox & Wyman Ltd, Reading
Filmset in Linotron Palatino by
Rowland Phototypesetting Ltd
Bury St Edmunds, Suffolk

To the Friends of my Friend,
Omar Torrijos,
in Nicaragua, El Salvador
and Panama

CONTENTS

FOREWORD

1

In August 1981 my bag was packed for my fifth visit to Panama when the news came to me over the telephone of the death of General Omar Torrijos Herrera, my friend and host. The small plane in which he was flying to a house which he owned at Coclesito in the mountains of Panama had crashed, and there were no survivors. A few days later the voice of his security guard, Sergeant Chuchu, alias José de Jesús Martínez, ex-Professor of Marxist Philosophy at Panama University, Professor of Mathematics and a poet, told me, 'There was a bomb in the plane. I *know* there was a bomb in the plane, but I can't tell you why over the telephone.'

At that moment the idea came to me to write a short personal memoir, based on the diaries which I had kept over the last five years, as a tribute to a man whom during that time I had grown to love. But as soon as I had written the first sentences after the title, *Getting to Know the General*, I realized that it was not only the General whom I had got to know over those five years – it was also Chuchu, one of the few men in the National Guard whom the General trusted completely, and it was this bizarre and beautiful little country, split in two by the Canal and the American Zone, a country which had become, thanks to the General, of great practical importance in the struggle for liberation taking place in Nicaragua and El Salvador.

2

A friend asked me, as I was writing the closing passages of this book, 'But why this interest which you seem always to have shown in Spain and Spanish America? There was Mexico in *The Power and the Glory*, Paraguay in *Travels With My Aunt*, Cuba in *Our Man in Havana*, Argentina in *The Honorary Consul*, you visited President Allende in Chile. And now you've published *Monsignor Quixote* . . .'

It was a question which I found difficult, for the answer belonged in the dark cave of the unconscious. My interest went back much further than my visit to Mexico in 1938 to report on the persecution there. My second published novel, *Rumour at Nightfall*, which appeared in 1934, was set in Spain during the Carlist wars, although at the time of writing I had only passed one day in Spain when I was sixteen. Then I had visited Coruña from a liner which had stopped at Vigo on the way to Lisbon. I was keeping my Aunt Eva company. She was meeting my uncle in Lisbon on his way back from Brazil where he had a coffee company, and at Vigo I proposed to her that we visit the grave of General Sir John Moore, a distant family connection, killed in the famous retreat from the French to Coruña where he had been buried, 'darkly at dead of night, the sods with our bayonets turning', immortalized by the only poem remembered of an Irish clergyman, the Reverend Charles Wolfe. Nearly sixty years passed before I visited the grave again, on which the lines are carved, carrying *Monsignor Quixote* as an idea in my head.

Rumour at Nightfall was a very bad novel which I never wish to see reprinted, but my interest in writing of things Spanish went even further back. 'There was a novel,' I told my companion, 'which I began just after I left Oxford and luckily I never found a publisher. It was called *The Episode*. I had been reading the only book of Carlyle's which I ever managed to finish – the life of an unsuccessful would-be poet called John Sterling who, when he was a young man, got involved with Carlist refugees in

London. I have its first edition here on my shelves. I found it in Chichester a dozen years ago for ten shillings, but I've never reread it.' I took the book, published in 1851, down from its place and opened it at the Table of Contents. There I read, 'Part I. Chapter 8. Torrijos.' The name Torrijos stared up from the page and struck me like a signal from the dead.

I began to read again of those unfortunate Spaniards with whom Sterling and my imaginary young hero had involved themselves – 'Stately tragic figures, proud, threadbare cloaks; perambulating, mostly with closed lips, the broad pavements of Euston Square and the regions about St Pancras new church.' I read on: 'Of those poor Spanish exiles the acknowledged chief was General Torrijos, a man of high qualities and fortune, still in the vigour of his years, and in these desperate circumstances refusing to despair.'

The General Torrijos whom I had grown to love had been killed in the vigour of his years and I had been close to him in the desperate circumstances from which he suffered, the clos- ing stages of the long-drawn-out negotiations with the United States over the Panama Canal Treaty, and the disappoint- ing aftermath. He too had refused to despair and he even seriously contemplated a possible armed struggle between his tiny country and the great power which occupied the Zone.

But why, my friend persisted in her question, this interest of mine over so many years in Spain and Latin America? Perhaps the answer lies in this: in those countries politics have seldom meant a mere alternation between rival electoral parties but have been a matter of life and death.

In 1976 I had known little of the past history of Panama. After its separation from Spain early in the nineteenth century Panama had chosen of its own accord to join fortunes with what was then a greater Colombia than exists today. The new republic of Panama in the twentieth century was something quite different. It was the personal creation of Theodore Roosevelt, who was determined to ensure that de Lesseps's dream of a canal to join the Atlantic to the Pacific Ocean, which after ten years of work had ended in financial disaster, should become a reality under the protection and virtual ownership of the United States. At the time of de Lesseps's failure Panama was still a province of Colombia, separated from her parent state, as it is to this day, by mountains and jungle with no road between. It became the object of the United States to ensure that Panama became a so-called independent state, since the negotiations with Colombia over the Canal rights dragged on and on and had proved finally impossible.

So it was that on 13 June 1903 with White House approval the *New York World* published an extraordinary communiqué announcing a rebellion which had not yet taken place.

Information has reached this city that the State of Panama, which embraces all the Canal Zone, stands ready to secede from Colombia and enter into a Canal Treaty with the United States.

The State of Panama will secede if the Colombian Congress fails to ratify the Canal Treaty. A republican form of Government will be organized. This plan is said to be easier of execution as not more than a hundred Colombian soldiers are stationed in the State of Panama.

Easy of execution it certainly proved, and the consequence was to saddle Panama with the personal rule of the Arias family and the oligarchy related to them, which lasted almost entirely to the benefit of the United States for more than half a century.

The rebellion, if rebellion it could be called, was finally organized by a French engineer, Bunau-Varilla, a left-over from de Lesseps's failed enterprise. He had the aid of Doctor Amador, a doctor belonging to the American-built railway which linked the Atlantic to the Pacific – a key position as it turned out, for when Colombia, aware of what was brewing, sent reinforcements of two hundred men to Colón on the Atlantic, the railway directors, after talking to Doctor Amador, found themselves conveniently unable to cope with the transport of so many men to Panama City – all they could manage was a small special train to accommodate the Colombian General Tokar, his aides and their wives, who were thus transported, without any of their troops, in comfort to the Pacific. There they were given a very friendly greeting and an excellent lunch, and were afterwards escorted to the lock-up.

The troops had landed on 2 November 1903, and on 6 November the United States recognized the independent Republic of Panama. The first Canal Treaty, establishing an American Zone on both sides of the future Canal in return for a derisory rent based on the tolls, was signed by the American Secretary of State Hay and the Frenchman Bunau-Varilla in Washington. It was thought unnecessary to ask for any Panamanian signature.

The Treaty, which was at intervals to bedevil the relations between Panama and the United States from 1903 till 1977, granted to the United States in perpetuity all rights and authority in the Canal Zone 'which it would possess if it were sovereign of the territory'. And although Panama by that mysterious 'if' could be said to retain a nominal sovereignty, Panamanians living or working in the Zone were subject to American law and to trial in the United States right up to the signing of the new Treaty in 1977. It was possible at many points to enter the Zone by crossing from one side of the street to the other. But if you were a Panamanian you had to exercise caution, for if you were involved in a traffic offence on the wrong side of the street, you would be judged in an American court by American law.

The Canal was completed just before the outbreak of the First

World War. It became the formal duty of every Panamanian president to protest against the terms of this treaty, which had been signed by a Frenchman without authority on behalf of the self-elected junta, but under the rule of the Arias family – Tomás Arias had been a member of the original junta – this was only a ritual and so it was regarded by the United States. In the end it was the demonstrators in the streets, not the Panamanian government, who gained some small concessions.

In 1959 after a serious riot President Eisenhower agreed that the Panamanian flag might be flown alongside the American at one spot where the Zone and free Panama touched. As a result of hostile demonstrations, a wire fence had been raised along a part of the Zone. Then in 1961 President Kennedy agreed that the Panamanian flag might be flown in the Zone wherever the American flag was displayed, over hospitals, over the Zone offices and over the canal locks. More than half a century of negotiations had achieved this small concession to national pride, but the American authorities minimized the victory as far as the schools in the Zone were concerned by ordering that no flags at all should be flown there.

Then one day in 1964 the children of one American high school raised the Union flag, and two hundred Panamanians marched into the Zone to hoist their own flag beside it according to the agreement. In the mêlée that followed the Panamanian flag was torn in pieces. It was then that the Panamanians showed to their own pacific government the violence of which they were capable. The border fence was torn down, the Panama City railway station, which was in the Zone, was attacked, shops were looted, and the riots spread all the way across the country to the Atlantic at Colón. The Marines were called out, and in the three days of fighting that followed eighteen Panamanians were killed, mainly in the poor area of El Chorillo where the main street in Panama City has been renamed the Avenue of the Martyrs. The National Guard played no part at all. They were confined to barracks.

It was a victory of a kind for the Panamanian people. A year later President Johnson announced that the old Treaty would be abrogated and negotiations would be opened for a new and fairer one, but eleven years later in 1976, when I was first invited to visit Panama, the negotiations were still going on. The leaders of Panama, however, had changed. In 1968 two young colonels of the National Guard, Torrijos and Martínez, had put President Arias on to an aeroplane for Miami and taken power. The following year Colonel Martínez, a right-winger, found himself conducted in a similar fashion on to a plane for Miami. Colonel Torrijos had taken over the National Guard and nothing would ever be quite the same again.

PART I

1976

1

In the winter of 1976 I was surprised and a little mystified to receive a telegram in Antibes from Panama signed by a certain Señor V – a name strange to me – telling me that I had been invited by General Omar Torrijos Herrera to visit Panama as his guest and that a ticket would be sent to me at the flight bureau of my choice.

To this day I don't know what had been in the mind of the General when the invitation was dispatched, but I felt no hesitation in accepting. I had quite forgotten that General Torrijos who had so nearly involved John Sterling in a perilous enterprise, but I knew that Panama, more even than Spain, had persistently haunted my imagination. As a child I had watched a pageant play written by Stephen Phillips in which, on the big stage of Drury Lane, Drake was shown attacking a very realistic mule train as it passed by on the gold route from Panama City to Nombre de Dios and I knew much of Newbolt's good-bad poem *Drake's Drum* by heart.

> Drake he's in his hammock an' a thousand mile away,
> (Capten, art tha sleepin' there below?)
> Slung atween the round shot in Nombre Dios Bay . . .

What did it matter that Newbolt's poem was inaccurate and that it was in Portobelo Bay, a few miles distant from Nombre de Dios, that Drake's body was sunk into the sea?

For a child the glamour of piracy lay around Panama in the story of how Sir Henry Morgan attacked and destroyed Panama City, and when I was older I had read of the disastrous Scottish settlement on the edge of the deep jungles of Darién, which remain to this day for the greater part pathless and unchanged.

ıne was to come when in the city of David I noticed that a
ᴊack security guard of General Torrijos had the name Drake
pinned on his shirt.

For amusement I asked him, 'Are you a descendant of Sir
Francis Drake?'

'Perhaps, ma'an,' he replied with a wide grin of pleasure, and
I recited part of Newbolt's poem to him.

'I've done it at last,' I thought at that moment, 'I really am
here in Panama.'

I had by this time seen what little was left of the gold route,
and soon I would be visiting Nombre de Dios, now only an
Indian village with no access by road even for a mule, and I
already felt oddly at home in this small remote country of my
dreams, as I had never felt in any country of Latin America
before. Another year, and it would seem quite natural for me to
be travelling to Washington carrying a Panamanian diplomatic
passport as an accredited member of the Panamanian delegation for the signing of the Canal Treaty with the United
States. One of the great qualities of General Torrijos was his
sense of humour.

2

After sending my reply I consulted my friend Bernard
Diederich, whom I had known in Haiti and the Dominican
Republic. He was now the *Time* correspondent for Central
America. In his reply he advised a certain caution towards
Señor V, who was apparently one of the General's counsellors,
and he proposed to come from Mexico City where he now lived
with his Haitian wife and his children to meet me in Panama.

I chose to fly from Amsterdam direct to Panama in order to
avoid changing planes in the United States, where I used to
have visa trouble, and I little thought how familiar I would
become with the long route of over fifteen hours – Amsterdam
to Panama City with three halts between.

For the first time in many years, since I had been over-saturated by air travel to Africa, Malaya and Vietnam, I felt again a certain sense of adventure. Why otherwise would I have made trivial notes in a diary from the moment I arrived in Amsterdam?

The city was well enough known to me from the period in 1946 when I would go there frequently in my role as a publisher to repurchase English paper which had been exported from England where it was rationed, paper which we badly needed to print our bestsellers – the Bible and the novels of a certain American lady called Mrs Parkinson Keyes whose books I found quite unreadable. I would pay my hotel bill in those days, or at least a large part of it, in cigarettes which I passed to the barman at the Hotel Amstel. There were lavish dinners and a lot of Bols gin drunk with printers and their wives and I soon learnt that the comradely thing to do was to slap my hostess's back-side as she sat down.

Schiphol Airport is surely one of the most comfortable airports in the world. On the ground floor there seems to be a sofa for every passenger, and three competing diamond shops (one of them advertising itself in Japanese) add to the air of leisure and luxury. Thanks to General Torrijos I was travelling first class so that I had the use of the Van Gogh lounge with its deep armchairs and heavily laden buffet. Even several hours of waiting passed pleasantly in those surroundings, and by the time I got on the plane I felt unusually happy, especially as I prefer Bols to any other gin.

'Young or old Bols?' an air hostess asked me as soon as we had taken to the air.

'Which is best?'

'I don't know, but my father – and he's as old as you are – prefers the young.'

I tried both and I disagreed with her father. I stuck to the old Bols all the way to Panama.

The sense of excitement grew, and a sense of fun which I had never known when I flew out to the French war in Vietnam, to

21

the Emergency in Malaya, the Mau Mau rebellion in Kenya, a leper colony in the Congo. These had been serious journeys – this one was not. I thought of it as only a rather comic adventure, inspired by an invitation from a complete stranger which had come to me out of the blue.

Fear can be easily experienced, but fun is hard to come by in old age, so I already felt a sense of gratitude to General Omar Torrijos. His title in Panama, I learnt later, was Chief of the Revolution, and he was the real ruler of the country. The only privilege of the President, so far as I could make it out on that first voyage, was to have a reserved parking place for his car at the Hotel Panama.

The sense of fun, however, faded on arrival. Two polite strangers met me at the airport – the dubious Señor V, they told me, was for a day or two in New York, but his car was at my disposal. They took me to the Panama Hotel (the name, alas, is changed now to the Hilton) and left me in a bedroom sixty feet long (I paced it out). No Diederich was there to greet me and I felt very much alone as I had little Spanish with which to communicate. In Mexico nearly forty years before I had been able, after twenty Berlitz lessons, to manage the present tense, though the future and the past were beyond my powers, but now even the present tense was mostly forgotten. I was beginning to feel shy of the mysterious General who was my host and rather foolish in this enormous room.

I turned my watch back, and as it was only breakfast time in Panama and I had already lunched on the plane, I tried to sleep. Señor V's chauffeur woke me – he didn't speak a word of English and I asked him to come back at 2.30 Panama time, indicating the figures on my watch. Diederich, I had been informed at the airport, was due from Mexico at one. The chauffeur came promptly back at 2.30, but still there was no Diederich. I told the man to come back at ten the next day. I was feeling gloomy. All sense of adventure had gone and as for fun . . . I began to hate my enormous room.

At 3.30 I went downstairs and ordered what I thought was to

22

be a rum punch under a slowly revolving fan, but there was no alcohol in it at all. On the Pacific side of Panama they are not accustomed to rum punches, and in any case I discovered later I had used the wrong term. Only the planter's punch contained something stronger than a flavour. At four o'clock there was still no Diederich, and I tried in vain to sleep. Why had I left my home in Antibes and my friends and come to Panama where the hours moved so slowly, even though they no longer moved backwards?

Around five everything changed for the better. Diederich arrived. It was more than ten years since we had driven together along the frontier track (only maps called it an international road) between Papa Doc's Haiti and the Dominican Republic, which I needed to know in order to finish my novel *The Comedians*. Together too we had visited the Haitian guerrillas lodged in the abandoned lunatic asylum lent them by the Dominican government.

The years had not changed him. We drank whisky and gossiped, and although he could shed no light on the reason behind the General's invitation at least he could diminish the extent of my ignorance. Señor V, he told me, was an old Arias man and he didn't trust him. When the two young colonels of the National Guard ended over half a century of Arias family rule by putting the President on a plane to Miami, Señor V had remained behind and even after the right-wing Colonel Martínez had been dispatched to the same 'Valley of the Fallen' he still survived. There were, of course, other survivors. Torrijos, it seemed, was not a man to make a clean sweep. He was not ideologically fettered. For example, there was one journalist whom it was well to treat with extreme caution as he was another Arias man. Diederich gave a clear physical description of the man, short and stout, with a false bonhomie who laughed without cause, so that I easily recognized him next day when sure enough he didn't fail to turn up.

We turned to the political situation. 'And the negotiations for the return of the Canal Zone? How are they going?'

'Oh, they are dragging on as usual. The General's getting impatient. For that matter so are the Americans in the Zone.' The leading American agitator in the Zone, a policeman called Drummond, claimed that his car had been blown up by a bomb, and he was to lead a demonstration against any negotiation in three nights' time.

The telephone rang. It was one of the two men who had met me at the airport. The voice told me that the General was planning to visit some place in the interior the next day. Would I like to go with him? I asked if I could bring my friend Diederich. The speaker obviously knew the name, and he sounded doubt-ful, as though he distrusted the *Time* correspondent. However, he said he would inquire. A few minutes later he rang back. The General had replied, 'Señor Greene is our guest. He can bring whom he likes.' A car would fetch us next morning at ten.

3

Next day there was a small misunderstanding. A driver came to the hotel promptly at ten and asked for Señor Greene. Diederich and I drove off with him. After about ten minutes I became (I don't know why) suspicious of the route we were taking. I was right. It was the wrong car and I was the wrong Mr Greene. We had been, so it appeared, on the way to a new copper mine in the interior. Back to the hotel and the right car and the right chauffeur, very much the right chauffeur, for he became my guide, philosopher and friend and remains so to this hour. Professor José de Jesús Martínez, better known to all Panama as Chuchu, was sergeant in the General's security guard. He was a poet and a linguist who spoke English, French, Italian and German as well as Spanish. But to us then he was only an unknown sergeant, driving us to a house in the suburbs where the General preferred to stay, rather than in his own home, partly perhaps for security reasons, with his great friend Rory González, the director of the copper mine, who many years ago had befriended the young Lieutenant Torrijos of the National Guard when he was on duty up-country.

It was a small insignificant suburban house, only made to look out of the ordinary by the number of men in camouflage uniforms clustered around the entrance and by a small cement pad at the rear in place of a garden, smaller than a tennis court, on which a helicopter could land. Admitted to the house, we passed a life-sized china dog and sat down to wait for our host. A budgerigar hopped in silence to and fro in a cage, seeming to measure out time like an ingenious Swiss clock.

Two men presently joined us. They wore dressing-gowns and underpants, one had bare feet and one was in bedroom slippers, and I was doubtful which to address as General. They were both men in their forties, but one was plump with a youthful and untroubled face which I felt would last a lifetime, the other was lean and good-looking with a forelock of hair which fell over his forehead and give-away eyes (he was the one with bare feet). At this encounter what the eye gave away was a sense of caution, even of suspicion, as though he felt that he might be encountering a new species in the human race. I decided correctly that this was the General.

Through the next four years I got to know those eyes well; they came to express sometimes an almost manic humour, an affection, an inscrutable inward thought, and more than all other moods, a sense of doom, so that when the news of his death in a crashed plane came to me in France, with my bags packed for yet another flight to Panama – accident? bomb? – it was not so much a shock that I felt as a long-expected sadness for what had seemed to me over the years an inevitable end. I remember how I had once asked him what was his most recurring dream and without hesitation he had answered, 'La muerte.'

For a while there was desultory conversation, translated by Chuchu, polite and guarded conversation through which somehow a few facts emerged – that he was, like myself, the son of a schoolmaster and that he had run away from home at seventeen and gone to a military academy in El Salvador. Perhaps he was painting a self-portrait to the stranger whom he had been rash enough to invite to his country – for what reason he may well have been wondering now himself – as a plain simple man of action, which was very far from the truth. With a sidelong look at me he attacked intellectuals. 'Intellectuals,' he remarked, 'are like fine glass, crystal glass, which can be cracked by a sound. Panama is made of rock and earth.'

I won the first smile out of him when I said that he had probably only saved himself from being an intellectual by running away from school in time.

We passed on then to the subject of the Caribbean. He seemed to know that I had been to Cuba, Haiti, Martinique, St Kitts, Grenada, Barbados, the Dominican Republic, Jamaica. Why, he asked, this interest?

It was, I said, in a way a family interest, and I told him the story of my grandfather and my great-uncle, how my grandfather was sent out at fifteen to join his brother in the management of the family sugar plantation in St Kitts, how his brother died a few months after his arrival of yellow fever at the age of nineteen and was said to have left thirteen children behind him.

It was as though I had opened a door to the General's confidence. His whole manner eased. No one with a great-uncle like that could possibly be an intellectual.

My grandfather, after he had returned home to Bedfordshire, I went on, never shook off his memories of St Kitts and finally in old age he left his wife and children to return there and die. I described the two graves side by side which I had visited and the church which resembled an old English parish church.

Perhaps the General was thinking of my story when later that afternoon he remarked to me of his own country, 'When you find grass uncut in a village cemetery you know it is a bad village. If they don't look after the dead, they won't look after the living.' I think it was the nearest he ever came to a religious statement, unless one counts the dream he told me two years later. 'I dreamt I saw my father on the other side of the street. I

26

called out to him, "Father, what is death like?" and he started to cross the street in spite of the traffic and I shouted to warn him and then I woke up.'

The whole atmosphere had indeed changed. When I told the General that Señor V's chauffeur could speak no English he at once appointed Chuchu as my guide. 'He will take you anywhere you want. Forget Señor V.' And so during the next four years Chuchu was always there at the airport to meet me, and we did indeed literally go wherever I wanted, whether in Panama, Belize, Nicaragua, Costa Rica, whether the trips entailed a plane, a helicopter or a car.

That morning, however, Torrijos made the choice. He wanted to spend some hours in Contadora, one of the Pearl Islands, where the Shah of Iran was later to be held in a kind of house arrest with Chuchu as his guard before he was dispatched to Egypt and his death. At the airport we had to wait while the General's plane was prepared and two small children insisted on playing with Torrijos. I was to notice later that he had an odd attraction for children. They were going with their mother on the commercial flight, but, perhaps because she was a pretty young woman, Torrijos invited the three of them to join our party.

At the hotel where we were to lunch the General left us for a rendezvous, which I suspected, perhaps wrongly, to be an amorous one. After eating we drove round the island, of which a large part was still virgin forest, and presently Torrijos rejoined us. He seemed relaxed and I felt reasonably sure that I detected in his face 'the lineaments of gratified desire'. He was no longer on his guard against intellectuals. He even expressed his admiration for the novels of García Márquez and the poems of a certain romantic, but in Chuchu's eyes inferior, Spanish poet.

At that moment a beautiful Colombian tourist came up and spoke to him, telling him that she was a singer, and she acted on him like a glass of his favourite whisky, which I was to learn was Johnnie Walker's Black Label. I was not surprised when he told me a few days later that he had taken his plane to Colombia for a date with her at the airport at Bogotá.

After she left yet another child came up and thrust his father's visiting card into the General's pocket and demanded one of his in return and the General let him have his way, just as he allowed a fat journalist, whom I recognized from Diederich's description as the suspect survivor from the days of Arias, to intrude on our party. I could see the dislike on Chuchu's face, but the General continued to talk frankly, as though there were no potential spy present, of the negotiations with the United States. 'If the French had built the Canal as planned,' he said, 'de Gaulle would have returned it. If Carter does not restart the negotiations promptly, measures must be taken. The year 1977 is the year when our patience and their excuses will be exhausted.' He spoke as though Panama and the United States were equal powers, and in a way he believed it.

The General had good reason for impatience. He referred to the riots of 1964 when the National Guard stayed in their barracks and left the students in charge. The young officer Torrijos had watched the guards' inaction with a sense of shame. 'It is a good thing,' he said, 'that Vance is Carter's Secretary of State. He was in Panama City when the rioting began and we had to smuggle him out of his hotel into the Zone, so he knows what a Panama riot can be like. He was a very frightened man.' He added, 'If the students break into the Zone again I have only the alternative of crushing them or leading them. I will not crush them.' Then he made a remark which he was fond of repeating: 'I don't want to enter into history. I want to enter into the Canal Zone.' Well, he did enter it, though on terms not as satisfactory as he had hoped, and it is possible that he paid for his success with his life.

We are too apt to class together the generals of South and Central America. Torrijos was a lone wolf. In his diplomatic struggle with the USA he had no support from Videla of the Argentine, Pinochet of Chile, Banzer of Bolivia – the authoritarian generals who held their power with the aid of the United

States, and who only existed at all because in the eyes of the Americans they represented anti-Communism. Torrijos was no Communist, but he was a friend and admirer of Tito and he was on good personal terms with Fidel Castro who kept him supplied with excellent Havana cigars, the bands printed with his name, and gave him advice to be prudent, unwelcome advice which he followed with reluctance. His country had become a haven of safety for refugees from Argentina, Nicaragua and El Salvador, and his dream, as I was to learn in the years that followed, was of a social democratic Central America which would be no menace to the United States, but completely independent. However, the nearer he came to success, the nearer he came to death.

That sunny afternoon on Contadora, after the rendezvous in the hotel, he was happy and reckless in his conversation. It was only later that I thought I could read the premonition of death in his eyes – a death which was not only the end of his dream of moderate socialism but perhaps the end of any hope of a reasonable peace in Central America.

It was here on the island of Contadora that negotiations with the United States had for years dragged along their slow length. Once again a delegation was about to arrive for talks, as usual led by old Mr Elsworth Bunker, a former ambassador in South Vietnam: they were to stay for a week on this pleasant tourist island, where it had become a habit to hold the parleys, and then they would go home for another year. Not much was expected of them. Gloria Emerson in her admirable book on Vietnam wrote of Bunker, 'For seven years he had never faltered in supporting and augmenting American policy in Vietnam. He was thought of – in the kindest terms – as a fierce, cold, stubborn man. To the Vietnamese he was known as "the Refrigerator".'

29

4

Next day Diederich and I took the train which joins Panama City to Colón on the Atlantic side. The gold rush in the Forties to California had created the railway, which was built at the cost of thousands of lives.

The stations at both ends of the track were in the American Zone and the railway had a nostalgic appeal. It seemed to belong to an innocent American past. The railway officials wore wide-brimmed hats which might have dated from the Civil War, and during a leisurely progress in a steam train through the Zone from the Pacific to the Atlantic, with glimpses of lakes and jungle, we had the impression of going backwards in time. For a little while we belonged to the unhurried age of Victoria, and when we left the station at Cristóbal and, by passing from one side of the street to the other, left the Zone and re-entered the Republic at Colón, we were still in the nineteenth century, walking under the beautiful balconied wooden houses which the French built at the time of de Lesseps. They had degenerated into slums without losing their beauty.

We had made a rendezvous with Chuchu for lunch at the Washington Hotel, for we wanted to go back by car through the Zone, where a small section of the old gold trail still exists. Diederich had need of film and we stopped at a photographic store and asked the way to the hotel. 'You have only to go straight on to the end of the street,' we were told.

It was a very long street and a very empty one. Only an occasional lounging figure broke the solitude at a side street corner, and we had walked perhaps a few hundred yards when we came on a group of Panamanian police standing beside a police van. One of them asked us peremptorily, 'Where are you going?'

I wanted to give a rude response, but luckily Diederich spoke first. 'The Washington Hotel,' he said.

'Get in the van.'

A policeman sat down beside us. I had the impression that

we had been arrested, but why? We drove off down the long street.

'Where are we going?' I asked.

'To the Washington Hotel, of course.'

Only then did the officer explain. 'You shouldn't be carrying your camera like that,' he told Diederich. 'This is a very bad street for thieves. They are armed with knives and they are on the look-out for tourists with cameras. You wouldn't have got to the hotel.'

'Why didn't they warn us at the camera shop where we bought film?'

'Oh, probably they expected to get your camera very cheap from the thieves. We've had to kill one or two of them this week.'

I felt that, like Secretary of State Vance, we were learning a little about Panama, though I had been warned in advance by that best and frankest of all guide books, *The South American Handbook*: 'Mugging, even in daylight, is a real threat in both Colón and Cristóbal.'

The Washington Hotel looks out over the Atlantic with the classical beauty of its age – it was built in 1913 – the year when the American Canal was completed though not yet opened. I couldn't help feeling a little ashamed when we were delivered at the door by a police van, but shame soon passed with the help of an excellent planter's punch, for we were now on the Caribbean side of Panama, in the company of Chuchu.

Over lunch we learnt a little more of Chuchu's past. In 1968, when the *coup d'état* took place, he began to feel that as a professor of Marxist philosophy he might be in some danger, so he departed for France where he gained a degree in mathematics at the Sorbonne. When news reached him that the fascist colleague of Torrijos had in his turn been put on a plane to Miami, he returned to Panama. They would no longer accept him as a Marxist professor, but they made him a professor of mathematics instead. On a later occasion he showed me a short book he had published with the title, *The Theory of Insinity*.

'What on earth is insinity?' I asked.

'Oh, well, you see, I had lost a front tooth and when I was lecturing I found I was saying "insinity".'

But how, I asked, had he become a sergeant in the General's security guard?

The square Mayan features lit up with the pleasure of memory: he had told us with gleeful satisfaction that he was 50 per cent Mayan Indian, 30 per cent Spanish, 10 per cent Negro and a bit of a mixture for the 10 per cent which remained. He was interested in photography, he said, and he went once for a night to visit the camp of the Wild Pigs, a force specially formed by Torrijos for guerrilla fiighting in the jungle and the mountains, to take some pictures of them. He was woken at five in the morning by the tramp of the new trainees, a thousand strong, who were singing a defiant song against the United States. No one man had written the song. It was improvised a little by every new squad to go with the beat of the feet. The theme was this:

I remember that 9 January when they massacred my people, students armed only with stones and sticks, but I am a man now and I carry a gun. Give the order, my general, and we will go into the Zone, we will push them into the water, where the sharks can eat *mucho Yanqui, mucho Yanqui.*

> *Los botaron*
> *De Vietnam*
> *Los tenemos*
> *Ahora en Cuba*
> *Dalés Cuba*
> *Dalés duro*
> *Panamá*
> *Dalés duro*
> *Venezuela*
> *Dalés duro*
> *Puerto Rico*
> *Dalés duro*

He had recorded the song on a cassette which he now played to us. He was so exhilarated by the song that he went to the commanding officer and told him that he wanted to join the Wild Pigs. The officer said he was too old to stand the rigorous training, but that morning the General happened to visit the camp from the house he had nearby at Farallón on the Pacific shore and the officer said to him as a joke that a professor was there who wanted to enlist. The General spoke to Chuchu 'in a very mean way' and then gave orders to the officer, 'Let the old fool try.'

Try he did and survived the severity of the training. They wanted to make him an officer, but he refused – so the General appointed him as a sergeant in his security guard to be on duty out of the university term. I was soon to realize the great trust in which the General held him, a trust he didn't feel for his Chief of Staff, Colonel Flores. The General had a respect for literature and it helped that Chuchu was a poet as well as a mathematician and a professor. Torrijos even gave Chuchu permission to draw on his account, so that without openly involving the General he was able to help many a refugee who had escaped from Somoza in Nicaragua, from Videla in Argentina, or from Pinochet in Chile.

Chuchu remained faithful to Marxism, but his first fidelity was always to Torrijos in spite of the General's belief in social democracy which to Chuchu must have seemed a cup of very lukewarm tea. Once that year when the three of us were together and the eternal question of the Canal negotiations came up, Chuchu burst out, 'I want a confrontation, not a treaty,' and then looked nervously across at the General, where he lay resting in his hammock, as though he had suddenly remembered that he was in uniform with only a sergeant's stripes. The General replied quietly, 'I am of your opinion,' for the General's social democracy was never lukewarm. It was a dream, of course; if you like, a romantic dream.

There is a charisma which comes from hope – a hope for victory against odds – Castro and Churchill are obvious examples. Torrijos was totally unaware of his very different charisma – the charisma of near despair. To be only forty-eight and to feel time running out – not in action but in prudence: to be establishing a new system of government: to be edging slowly towards social democracy by means that required infinite patience (and yet in his travels he hadn't even the patience to take a canoe or wait for a bridge over a river – he would jump in and swim across): to live day by day with the Canal problem, dreaming, as a soldier, of the simple confrontation of violence and yet to act all the same with that damnable long-drawn-out prudence which Fidel Castro advised . . . it wasn't easy. He said to me once, 'And I thought when I had the power I would be free.'

Would he, I often wondered during the next four years, have the time to establish his social democracy? In England, I think, more than ever before, we are prepared to recognize other forms of democracy, even under a military chief of state, than our parliamentary one, which worked satisfactorily for about two hundred years in the special circumstances of those two hundred years. Panama had already evolved a very different form of democracy.

In the Assembly of the Panama Republic there were 505 representatives elected by regional votes. In order to stand for election a candidate had to have at least twenty-five letters of support. The elected representatives met only once a year for a month in the capital to report on their regions and to vote on legislation. The rest of the time they had to live with their constituents and their problems. (No mere weekend 'surgery' in the English fashion for them. I had an impression that there might well be a bigger turnover of representatives than of our MPs.) A Legislative Council of about fifteen members toured the regions during the year and discussed with the representatives the legislation on which the Assembly would vote. The representatives could belong to any political faith, but each one was meant to represent his region and not his party.

Ministers were appointed by the chief of state – Torrijos smiled when I said to him that a man could choose his enemies but not his friends, for he had a number of reactionaries among his ministers, chosen for tactical reasons. The General, like the members of his Legislative Council, was constantly on the move, listening to the complaints, taking with him the ministers concerned who had to reply to the people. The system might well work in Panama, a small country. It was closer to the democracy of the Athenian *agora* then to the democracy of the House of Commons, and not for that reason to be despised. It may even have been a step away from true democracy when, after the signing of the Treaty, to please the United States, the General formed his own party to fight an old-style parliamentary election with the old labels, Conservatives, Liberals, Socialists, Communists.

After we returned from Colón, I went to a typical meeting between electors and representatives in El Chorillo, one of the poorest sections of Panama City. The representative of El Chorillo spoke at inordinate length, and the electors' complaints reached down even to petty details like the slack behaviour of the man in charge of the local swimming baths. You could see how bored the General was by the way he twisted the cigar in his mouth – one of the good Havanas provided for him by Castro. I thought of all the hours of meetings like this which he must suffer as he moved around the country. Propaganda posters hung on the walls – 'Omar has his ideal – total liberation. They have not yet launched a projectile which can kill an ideal.' 'The country with a fifth frontier.' 'El Chorillo – the Avenue of the Martyrs.' (I remembered that it was in El Chorillo, which abuts on the Canal Zone, that eighteen students lost their lives in 1964.)

Everyone in the crowded hall was glad when the representative left the podium. The meeting sprang to life. A coloured girl, dragging an old silent woman in her wake, shrieked like a voodoo-possessed dancer and flung her arms around her head – the old lady, she told us, was seventy-six and still working for the government and she had no pension. The points of the speeches now were underlined by the drums of supporters and that made the scene even more like Haitian voodoo. A Negro speaker talked with great dignity and confidence: 'We have the moral authority of those who work for low wages.' Again and again the Zone cropped up in the speeches – 'We are waiting to go in, we are with you, you have only to give the order,' and all the drums rolled. The General no longer twisted his cigar.

An important complaint emerged. A number of high-rise flats had been built with the inevitable sabotage of lifts and windows that we have experienced in England and France. High-rise flats are for the rich who can escape to theatres and restaurants and parties, not for the poor who are condemned to live in isolation. Moreover, the charge for these flats was beyond the tenants' means, so that they were in debt. The General told his Minister of Housing to reply and a very bad job he made of it. The General asked for more information. A girl spoke up with anger, a woman had hysterics, the drums beat.

There were complaints next about the health service – the Minister of Health indignantly defended his doctors. He made a better impression than the Minister of Housing. A young magistrate demanded better security in the streets. The hours passed.

The General took his turn to speak, but not from the podium. He balanced on the giddy edge of the platform, a glass of water in his hand, a swim of faces close below him – not much security there. An officer of the National Guard sat immobile on the platform chewing gum like an American colonel.

The untrustworthy journalist who had joined us on the island elbowed his way to my side, and I asked him, 'Who is that officer?'

'He is Colonel Flores, the Chief of Staff. A very loyal man like his father before him. He too was very loyal.'

But loyal to whom, I wondered? Loyal to President Arias?

It was the General's first meeting in the slums of El Chorillo and El Chorillo was going to have its say. The faces might appear fierce and fanatical and angry but they were friendly. 'We know you very well, here, General. We see you driving by every week to buy your lottery ticket.' Laughter and the drums laughed too.

Afterwards a rumour was spread, by one who had attended the meeting and knew it was a lie, that the General was drunk with vodka (not his choice of drink) and had fallen off the platform. One chooses one's enemies . . .

That night I dined with Chuchu and one of his refugees – an Argentinian woman who had fled from the regime of Videla to the security of Panama. We had a not very good dinner (good meals were not common in Panama) beside the Pacific under a sky of stars with a bottle of Chilean wine. 'It has to be of the years before Pinochet, an Allende year,' Chuchu demanded of the waiter, and I felt happy and at home, and my happiness was only a little diminished by the thought of how brief my stay was to be. I little thought that I would be returning and returning and returning . . .

Next evening it was a very different demonstration which I attended in the Canal Zone.

The long negotiations which were trying the patience of Torrijos were proving not nearly slow enough to satisfy the inhabitants of the Zone. To them any negotiation at all was treasonable.

Panama is not the Canal, and the Zone was a whole world away from Panama. You could tell the difference the moment you entered the Zone from the neat well-built unimaginative houses and the trim lawns. There seemed to be innumerable golf courses and you felt the jungle had been thrown back by a battalion of lawn mowers.

> And the wind shall say: here were decent godless people:
> Their only monument the asphalt road
> And a thousand lost golf balls.

Not quite godless, however. In the telephone book of the Zone I counted more than fifty churches – some of them of Christian sects quite unknown to me before. Perhaps as sects multiply, belief diminishes. I also read in the telephone book very re-assuring information of what to do in the event of a nuclear attack without warning.

Your first warning of an attack might be the flash of a nuclear explosion. If outdoors, take cover instantly in any building, or behind a wall, or in a ditch or culvert, or even under an automobile. By getting inside or under something (within seconds) you might avoid serious burns or injury from the heat or blast waves.

If no cover is available lie down on your side, curl up, cover your head with your arms and hands. Never look at the flash or the fire-ball.

If indoors go to the strongest part of the building (usually in the central area, first floor, protected by inner walls) and keep low.

Move to an approved fall-out shelter as soon as the heat blast ends for protection from radio-active fall-out which will arrive later.

The same curious lack of any sense of reality marked the demonstration in the Zone.

The demonstration was held in a large stadium only a few hundred yards away from the hall in El Chorillo where the drums had played. The American police officer, Mr Drummond, was intended to be the star. He had personally issued a writ on constitutional grounds against President Ford and Kissinger for holding talks on a new treaty without first getting the approval of Congress. Then his car had been destroyed by a bomb, so he claimed, in mysterious circumstances. This had given me the impression of a highly dangerous man whose life was at risk, an impression not borne out by the demonstration. Mr Drummond had the thinnest legs, band-aged in tight brown trousers, of any man I have ever seen. When he stood up to speak – very uninspiringly – to a rather small and highly respectable audience, one leg seemed to lean against the other for support, or perhaps to make music like a grasshopper.

Isolated by the arc lights, he was supported in the middle of the stadium by a little group of men and women who looked like a committee elected to arrange a Christmas entertainment. They spoke in turn, throwing back at El Chorillo *their* slogans, but unaided by drumbeats the voices seemed to get lost in the night air before they reached the meagre audience. Only one blue-haired old lady, like a Universal Aunt, got some energy into her phrases – 'God and country . . .' 'Eighth wonder of the world . . .' 'We left our country and our home life . . .' 'No desire to live under a repressive form of government . . .' 'The Canal can't be worked without a US Zone and US laws . . .' 'The Zone's got to be incorporated into the Union like the Virgin Islands.' The audience cheered occasionally but not very often, usually when a speaker attacked a member of his own government. Christian names were used like pejoratives, as though there had been treachery in the family. 'Gerry' was a traitor, 'Henry' was a traitor. 'In 1975 a secret agreement was made between Henry and Torrijos.' They could find no term bad enough to describe the State Department, perhaps because it hadn't got a Christian name.

The protesters looked very lost and lonely in the vast stadium and the hot and humid night, and one felt a little sorry for them. God and Country would almost certainly let them down just as surely as Gerry and Henry had done. A young woman asked the audience to send letters and 'clippings' to members of Congress. 'I can supply you with their telephone numbers.' She wasn't as impressive as the Negro in El Chorillo. Buckets stood around for contributions to help Mr Drummond's suit against Henry and Gerry, and the audience was asked to go into the arena to sign a petition, but not many went.

These people too looked on 1977 as a critical year, but confrontation in their eyes was a simple affair of flying in reinforcements from Fort Bragg in North Carolina to aid the 10,000 troops already in the Zone. They had been encouraged by the mildness of some riots the previous October which perhaps had been provoked in order to prove to Henry and Gerry that Panama was ungovernable. They didn't know that the General had received fifteen days' advance warning of what was planned from a CIA agent who squealed. As a result forty students were lodged for the day in prison where the General lectured them on the true nature of political and economic problems, and then they were released.

6

The next day my friend Diederich left for his home in Mexico, and Chuchu and I began to plan a journey together through the interior of Panama. I suspected that a rumour of our project would reach Señor V. When I went to see the General at the house of Rory González (Torrijos wanted to know my reactions to the meeting in El Chorillo and I gave them as frankly as I have written them here – even to the doubts about his Chief of Staff), our conversation was interrupted by Señor V on the telephone. He demanded to know what my travel plans were. I was evasive. My intentions, I said, altered every hour – I wanted to drift with the wind. He insisted that I should dine with him that night and together we would work out a programme. A programme was essential. I would of course take his car . . .

'I have Chuchu's car.'

'But his car has been bombed.'

That was true – Chuchu had told me the car had blown up outside his house when his son turned on the engine, though luckily only the car suffered injury.

'The General has lent him one of his.'

It did occur to me several times on our journey that the General's car might well prove a more enticing target.

I told the General what was happening: I told him how much I disliked making a programme with Señor V. Torrijos was in a very good humour (perhaps because he was flying off next day to his rendezvous at Bogotá airport). He agreed at once that any programme was detestable. I should go off with Chuchu where

I wanted and forget all about Señor V. 'If he proposes anything,' he said, 'do the opposite.'

Chuchu and I had lunch at the Marisco. The proprietor, a Basque, was a friend of his and yet another refugee – a veteran refugee this time, from Franco. I was still thirsty in the heat and the humidity and I longed for a rum punch, but the Basque didn't even know what a rum punch was and when his barman was consulted he couldn't make one, he said, because he had no milk. Milk?

Later driving through the streets of old Panama, Chuchu stopped to speak to a black on the pavement. 'He was one of my pupils,' he said, 'when I was a Marxist professor.' Perhaps to show what a good professor he had been he asked the man, 'Who was Aristotle?'

'The first Venezuelan philosopher,' the black replied without hesitation. For a while after that Chuchu drove in thoughtful silence.

I had that night dinner with Señor V at a restaurant called Sarti's – an elegant one by Panama standards – but it was an uncomfortable situation and not helped at all by the barman's non-alcoholic idea of what a rum punch should be. I admitted that Chuchu and I intended to drive up to David, the second largest town on the Pacific side. 'I will join you in David,' Señor V said.

'Or perhaps we may go instead to Taboga,' I added hastily. 'We haven't decided yet.'

Taboga is a small island in the Pacific where no cars are allowed – it sounded to me an ideal place to work.

'I'll join you there then,' he said.

He went on to demand that I warn him in advance whenever I had an appointment to see the General. He wanted to be present, he said, in order to study the growth of our relationship, and he told me that he intended to issue to the press some photographs taken on Contadora of the two of us, but here I was firm. 'You can't do that. The General has said that they are not to be released until after I leave.'

'If you go to David,' he said, 'you must tell Chuchu to report at every guard post on the way. I want to be kept informed of where you are.'

7

So much that happened in Panama during the next four years proved as unexpected as the events in a dream. The Republic was to me an unknown land, and my voyage there was a voyage of discovery, and the first discovery was the Haunted House. Chuchu and I had driven over the Bridge of the Americas where we could see the ships lined up to take their turn to enter the Canal and pass towards the Atlantic; we had driven through the American Zone and re-entered Panama. There were no frontier posts to distinguish one from another, but the Haunted House was undeniably in Panama. Nothing could have been less American than the bar next door, decorated with cabalistic signs and bearing a name in Spanish meaning The Bewitched. The barman told us that the adjoining house had not been occupied for forty years. The owner of the house and bar was an old man who lived in Panama City. He would neither sell the house nor let it. Yes, the barman agreed, the superstitious believed it to be haunted.

'By a ghost?'

'By a woman screaming.'

'Can we look round the house?'

There was nothing to be seen, the barman assured us. The house was quite empty and anyway we would have to get permission from the owner.

When could we see him?

If we came back to the bar on a Sunday we would certainly find him. He came always on a Sunday.

'Tell him,' Chuchu said with the authority of his sergeant's stripes, 'that we will be back next Sunday.'

We left the bar and took a closer look at the house: an ugly square building with no character but its secrecy and its security. There were steel shutters on the already heavy doors and the windows were barred as well as shuttered. Only a hole, the size of a half-crown, in one of the doors gave us a view within. The house was certainly not completely empty – I could just make out in the obscurity two pictures and a cupboard. To me the house smelt of an old crime. A woman's scream? 'We have to see inside,' I told Chuchu.

'On the way back,' he said, but a year was to pass before I had my way. It proved easier getting to know the General than the interior of the Haunted House.

We drove on towards Santiago with the intention of stopping for a while at a small town called Antón where Chuchu said there was a miraculous image of Christ. Not that Chuchu believed in the Christian God – he was too good a Marxist for that – though he believed in the Devil. 'Haven't you noticed,' he said, 'when you try to open a swing door, you always begin by pushing it the wrong way? That's the Devil.' He was proud of his Mayan blood and he half believed in the Mayan gods. He told me that once in a museum he had talked to a Mayan idol and he knew he was understood. It was just a question of catching the right note. As he drove he gave an imitation of the note, which startled me. It was more like a shriek than a prayer. He had a small Mayan idol in his house and he was anxious to give it me so that there would always, he said, be a radiation of Maya in my home.

I much preferred it when he recited Rilke in German, or one of the Spanish poets whom he admired, and I tried to respond with a few lines of Hardy and with Baudelaire's L'Invitation au voyage; he preferred the French to the English in spite of my accent. English, he said, was not a poetic language, and Shakespeare was much inferior to Calderón. However, he approved of Newbolt's poem Drake's Drum. 'Slung atween the round shot in Nombre Dios Bay . . .' He promised to take me to Nombre de Dios. It was impossible to go by road – there was no

43

road: we would have to borrow an army plane – no, a plane couldn't land there – a helicopter. The General would certainly lend us one.

It was later on this trip that I discovered a poem which he could really appreciate and one of the few which I knew by heart, Yeats's *An Irish Airman Foresees his Death*. Chuchu had a small second-hand aeroplane which at the moment was undergoing repairs and there were lines in the poem he made me repeat more than once.

> I know that I shall meet my fate
> Somewhere among the clouds above.
>
> A lonely impulse of delight
> Drove to this tumult in the clouds.

As a Marxist he approved of:

> My country is Kiltartan Cross,
> My countrymen Kiltartan's poor.

Once in a Panama bar he made me put the lines on to tape.

We passed several National Guard posts on our way to Antón, but he made no telephone calls to Señor V. He said, 'If he comes to David to find us, we will have gone. We won't spend a night there.'

At Antón we couldn't get into the church to see the miraculous Christ. The church was locked and no one seemed to know where the priest was. 'Never mind,' said Chuchu. 'On the way back.' It was the second time he had used the phrase and suddenly in my mind it became the title of a novel which, alas, I was never to write.

As he drove I began to learn a little about Chuchu's family life. He had a rather vague number of children by several women and he supported nearly all of them, though a boy and a girl were with their mother, his divorced wife, in the States. This wife had left him for an American professor and he spoke of her always with regret. I never knew what had happened to an earlier wife – the mother of the boy in the bombed car. He

44

had a girl living with him now. She was only a poor thing, he said, and he sheltered her out of pity. He couldn't turn her out as 'the rich woman' wanted. He would like to be rid of 'the poor thing' all the same . . .

It was the first I had heard of the rich woman. By the rich woman, he told me, he had had a baby girl. The mother was a fellow poet. 'If I go and see her we always sleep together, but she says I only come because of the food in her fridge.'

We stopped at the cantonment of the Wild Pigs, near the General's small house on the Pacific. Chuchu had nostalgic memories of his training there and we encountered the first friend he had made in the days when he was a middle-aged recruit. They must have been difficult days – being a professor among the Wild Pigs. He was even hit on the head once for reading a book. But this man had come up to him and said, 'Come and shit with me,' which was the greatest mark of friendship it was possible to offer.

Now Chuchu had become a great man in their eyes, even among the officers, for he was known to be the trusted companion of the General. There had been a colonel here, Sanjur, who started a rebellion in '69 after the General had exiled his fellow colonel and seized power. The General was at the time on a visit to Mexico, but he immediately took a plane back to David, to the consternation of the conspirators who thought that he would be content to follow President Arias and Colonel Martínez without fuss to Miami. From David he set off towards the capital and the rebellion collapsed. The junior officers were forgiven, Colonel Sanjur was imprisoned, but the CIA arranged his escape by bribery and took him to the Canal Zone.

Another Wild Pig buttonholed us in the camp. He needed money badly and for long he had day-dreamed of an occasion when the General would visit the camp and speak to him and he would find the courage to tell the General of his trouble. He had three children – well, he admitted to us, not three, it was really only two, but three sounded a lot better, he thought, and he was in genuine need of three hundred dollars. Three hundred? Well, of course, two hundred would satisfy him, but it was always well to ask for more than you actually needed.

The real object of Chuchu's visit to the camp was to get ammunition for a new acquisition of which he was very proud. He already had quite an arsenal at his home ready for confrontation next year with the *Yanquis* if it came to street fighting, but this was something special – a Russian repeating pistol which could be adjusted to fire from the shoulder. He had obtained it from a friend in the Cuban Embassy in exchange for a Belgian revolver. There was obviously magic to him in the mere word Russian. We would try it out, he promised, when we got to David.

When we reached Santiago we had a very bad meal at what appeared to be the only restaurant – a Chinese one. I was encouraged by the sight of a Gordon's bottle behind the bar and I ordered a gin, but whatever the bottle contained it wasn't gin. I said so and the Chinaman smiled and smiled. We chose for safety a very European dish, chop-suey, and I asked for some pimento sauce to cheer it up. The bottle certainly had the right label, but what it held was only coloured water, and when I complained the Chinaman smiled and smiled and smiled. The restaurant formed part of an hotel, but we thought it better to look elsewhere.

We found a motel and asked for two rooms. 'But where are the girls?' the proprietor asked with astonishment and suspicion.

Chuchu took off his revolver belt and laid his revolver on his bedside table with the safety catch raised. 'A precaution?' I asked and often later back in France I had reason to recall the aphorism with which he replied, 'A revolver is no defence.' He was indeed a wise man. Even the motel's doors proved, as he had said, that the Devil existed.

On the road to David Chuchu was in high spirits, casting a glance back from time to time as though his sight could penetrate the boot where the beloved Russian pistol rested. He told me a bizarre story of one of his last visits to David. The Dean of Guatemala University, an honoured guest of Panama, was with him – also a bottle of whisky which the Dean had emptied while Chuchu drove. The Dean was quite drunk by the time they arrived and for some reason all the hotels were full, so they went to the police station to beg a cell for the night, but the cells were full too. There remained the little square with its stone benches, but the benches were all occupied by fourteen homosexuals. Luckily Chuchu was in uniform. He ordered a *guardia* to summon the homosexuals before him and after giving them a long reproving address he dismissed them to their homes. Then he and the Dean were able to sleep on the benches in the empty square.

In David we went to the barracks of the National Guard, so that Chuchu could leave the General's car in safety for the night, for he remembered the bomb which had damaged his own. There we found Captain Wong. Captain Wong was much interested in the Russian weapon. He took his own American model and led us to a rifle range. The American repeater worked perfectly. The Russian spluttered out a few bullets and stuck. Another try. No trouble with the American weapon and the Russian stuck again. Chuchu was furious, injured, humiliated. It was almost as if he had been betrayed by a woman he loved. To think that he had given a good Belgian revolver in exchange for the Russian gun at the Cuban Embassy . . . It was as though the prophet Marx himself had failed him.

I heard Chuchu tell Captain Wong that we should see him again 'on the way back' – Captain Wong, the miraculous Christ, the Haunted House, all were promised on the way back and my projected novel with that title again emerged from the shadows. In my book the promised return would never be fulfilled – there would be no going back for my chief character.

Chuchu was silent and sad as we drove up next day into the mountains towards a village called Boquete, for he was brooding on his Russian repeater, but to me it was like a return to life after a long sickness – the malignant sickness of a writer's block. I was coming to the end of *The Human Factor*, an abandoned novel which I had picked up again in desperation to escape just such a block. Five years had passed after the previous novel and I was beginning to feel already the menace of another long block when *The Human Factor* too would be gone and leave my mind empty.

But with *On the Way Back* everything seemed to be possible: my writing days, I thought, were not over after all. The main elements of the story and the characters were already assembling – the dangerous situation between Panama and the States: Chuchu himself: the bomb in his car: the expression he had used in the motel – 'A revolver is no defence': his proof of the Devil's existence: the Dean of Guatemala University and the fourteen homosexuals: impressions were clustering like bees round a queen on this journey we were taking together. It was for that reason I found myself happy all the way to Boquete, a charming little town nearly three thousand feet up the slopes of a volcano. The streets were full of the sound of rushing water, and the air was as fresh as the air in a Swiss village, even the small hotel was pretty, and so was the hostess who had the grace and the looks of a young Oona Chaplin.

8

Next day we visited the great copper mine, managed by Rory González, the General's friend. It was a new State acquisition and believed then to be the great hope for Panama's future, which otherwise depended on banking, flags of convenience, sugar, coffee and yucca, apart from the wretchedly small income received by the terms of the old treaty for the use of the Canal which was already incapable of taking the largest boats – the oil tankers and the aircraft carriers. The concession for working the mine had been bought from a Canadian interest: the mine was not expected to be in production for another four years, and it was to prove a very chancy gamble.

The mine, I was told, was the largest in the world, larger even than the great mine in Chile at Chuquicamata which I had visited when Allende was President, but the copper had value for its quantity rather than its quality. A Canadian who belonged to the former management was naturally pessimistic about the chances – he didn't want to be proved wrong – he wanted failure. He didn't believe that the mine could be in full production before 1986 to '88, and what would be the price of copper then? An assessment of the copper prices was no more reliable than a newspaper horoscope. Japan had formed big reserves of copper when her balance of payments was favourable and she might sell off these reserves at any time.

We penetrated as far as the tunnelling into the mine had gone, we had lunch in the canteen, and a young Englishman made a mysterious remark to me, 'To be superstitious brings bad luck.' (Had I tossed some salt over my shoulder?) I noted in my diary for an unknown reason the presence of 'a tired American', but he has left no memory behind him. Then we were back on the road to Boquete again.

Chuchu's melancholy had quite gone. He sang and he recited poems and he quoted a cynical Panamanian phrase one could use to a girl, which stuck, I don't know why, in my mind – 'Come with me to be alone.' It is odd what you remember and what you forget. There were unfamiliar birds and unfamiliar butterflies, and by the wayside the Indian faces of a tribe which might be threatened by the copper mine, for if it were a success it would change the whole pattern of the tribe's life. A horseman rode by carrying a cock on his hand in the way a waiter carries a tray.

When I went to bed I entered in my diary a note for the new novel, little thinking that it would never be written: 'Start novel with a girl from a French left-wing weekly interviewing the General. She's escaping the pain of an unsatisfactory marriage in Paris and wants to avoid further pain. In the end she goes back to her pain and not to happiness.'

Next day we returned to David in order to catch a plane to the island of Bocas del Toro, a depressed banana port (just how depressed I was to find out only several years later). I had become attracted to it because it was the furthest point west that Columbus reached off the coast of Panama, and perhaps because the *South American Handbook* stated with its habitual frankness, 'No tourist ever goes there.'

As we drove I told Chuchu of the novel which I was planning, and perhaps that is the reason why it never came to be written beyond the first chapter. To tell a story is much the same as to write it – it is a substitute for the writing. 'You and the French-woman journalist are the main characters,' I told him. 'The General puts you in charge of her to show her the country. He lends you one of his cars, and you go off together, just as we have done. Always there are things you can't see – like the miraculous Christ and the Haunted House. "On the way back," you repeat, and that will be the title of the book. But the irony is that neither of you will take the road back.'

'We make love together?' Chuchu demanded with a certain eagerness.

'Oh, the idea grows in your head, but she's not like the other women you have known. You have fears and scruples. All the same by the time you reach David or some town still further off, you both know that it's going to happen. You stop outside a hotel, and by mutual consent, without a word being said between you, you take one room. She wants to wash off the dust of the road and brush her hair. You tell her you must leave the General's car with the National Guard for safety and then you will return . . . and make love of course, but both of you know that without speaking of it. She washes and does her hair. She's happy at the thought that all the hesitations are at last over. The decision has been made. But you don't come back. She waits for you in vain. During the few moments you were with her in the room someone has planted a bomb in the car which goes off. She hears the explosion while she brushes her hair, but she thinks it is only your car backfiring . . .'

'Am I killed?' Chuchu asked with excitement, and I remembered how he had told me earlier that day, 'I am never going to die.'

'Yes. Do you mind being killed in a novel?'

'Mind?' He bared his arm. His skin had risen in lumps. 'You must write it. Promise you'll write it.'

'I'll try.' But the book was never written, and it was the General and not Chuchu who died.

We missed our plane to Bocas at David, but Chuchu showed no sign of disappointment. 'When you come back,' he said – it was a variant of 'on the way back' and a variant which I didn't believe, for I saw no reason why I should ever return to Panama.

We called again on Captain Wong and drove with him to the outskirts of the town where a car had been abandoned by thieves to rust away. Captain Wong had decided on some more firing practice, with revolvers this time. (The Russian pistol was left in the boot.) The target chosen was the number plate of a car which contained the letters O and I.

'We aim for the centre of the O,' Captain Wong decided. Unfortunately after firing three shots each they had not even touched the number plate. Perhaps my eyes showed a trace of amusement for Chuchu held out his revolver and said, 'All right. You try.'

'I'm no good. I won't even hit the car. Why waste good ammunition?'

'No, no. Try.'

I fired. I didn't get into the O but by an odd fluke I dotted the I. We got back into the car in silence.

Chuchu and I left David and started on our road towards Panama City. At Antón we did at least succeed in seeing the miraculous image. The wooden Christ was covered in gold ornaments which had apparently led some thieves to steal it, but as they were carrying it out of the church the weight of the ornaments miraculously increased, so that they were forced to abandon the statue.

Perhaps because I was travelling with an imaginary woman as well as Chuchu and I needed to watch them together, I felt unwilling to return yet to Panama City. It was Sunday. I

51

reminded him that we had a date at the Haunted House. But mysteriously the bar was closed, an incomprehensible event to the neighbours, for on a Sunday all the bars are open everywhere. I became more determined than ever to return one day and see inside. Was the old man afraid of the inquisitive stranger in uniform?

Disappointed, we turned towards Ocú, a little town famous according to Chuchu for its leather sandals. In Ocú Chuchu bought enough leather for two pairs and we asked a peasant to whom we had given a lift where we could have the sandals made. He assured us he was as good as any sandal-maker in the region and he guided us to his hut.

Chuchu had already told me of the unusual drinking habits in Panama, habits followed usually even by the General. 'We are drunkards,' Chuchu said. 'On Sundays we drink in order to get drunk, but we don't drink during the week. You in Europe are alcoholics. You drink all the time.' I'm glad that during our days together he chose to follow the European custom.

Our peasant, however, proved to be quite sober. He brought two chairs out into the yard of his hut and began work watched by eleven children and a pregnant girl. At first he soaked the leather and then modelled it around the foot and cut it. Suddenly there were cries of 'Uahu', followed by what sounded like the barking of dogs. Two neighbours arrived on the scene. They wore funny little hats with round rims which seemed to balance on their protuberant ears. They had been celebrating Sunday ever since their morning Mass. At first they just continued to bark (the General later corrected me – this was traditional peasant singing). Then one of them attached himself to me, sitting on the ground beside me holding my hand. He said he was only interested in *Religión*, and he wanted to talk about it. Was I a *gringo*? No, I wasn't a *gringo*. I was English. Was I *Católico*? Yes, I was *Católico*. Then we must talk about *Religión*.

I asked my friend what his priest was like. 'Too materialist,' he replied.

I tried to turn the conversation away from religion towards

52

politics and the Canal, but no one was interested in either.

'And the General?' I asked. 'Do you like the General?'

'Half good and half bad.'

'What is the bad half?'

'He doesn't like the *gringos*.'

'Why do you like the *gringos*?'

Four hundred men of the Peace Corps, whom Kennedy had sent to Panama, had been expelled by the General, but at least in this poor area near Las Minas one of them had made converts. 'He was a good man. He taught us things, and he drank with us always on Sundays.' I seemed to be in another country, very distant from the slum dwellers of El Chorillo and their belligerent cries or the song of the Wild Pigs.

It must have taken nearly two hours to have our sandals made. They were not very good sandals and I abandoned mine next day, leaving them behind in a bad hotel where there were too many large cockroaches in the dull town of Chitré. Chuchu was disappointed in me, the sandals were genuine home-made Panamanian (he might have been talking of shoes by Lobb of St James's), but I noticed that he didn't wear his own for very long either.

9

On our way to Panama City we stopped at Rio Hato where the Wild Pigs had their cantonment and the General was staying in his modest house close by on the Pacific. General Torrijos had with him that day Aquilino Boyd, the Foreign Secretary, and the members of his military staff who had gathered there because the American delegation and Mr Bunker were due to arrive next day. A little to my embarrassment because of what I had told him of Colonel Flores, the General insisted on intro-ducing me to the members of his staff, beginning with the Colonel, who was chewing gum as he had done at El Chorillo. In the hand which he reluctantly offered I thought I could detect his dislike and his disdain. For what reason, I could feel him demanding, could he, the Chief of Staff, be expected to greet a civilian and foreigner as an equal? But in the handshake of the intelligence officer I thought I detected a sympathy and a kind of connivance – an interesting contrast.

Chuchu and I bathed in the clean, clear, quiet water of the Pacific while the staff met, and afterwards we lunched very badly in the mess of the Wild Pigs, lingering there until the General had got rid of his military guests. Apparently he wanted to talk to me. The visit of the Americans seemed to weigh heavily on his mind, perhaps the thought of the endless haggling for a fair treaty which seemed never to reach a conclusion, and yet an open confrontation was denied him if he was to follow Castro's advice. He made an odd comparison which to this day I don't understand: 'You and I have something in common. We are both self-destructive.' He added quickly, 'Of course I don't mean suicidal.' It was as though at that moment he had opened for me a crack in the door of a secret room, a door which he would never quite close again.

He continued to talk of the confrontation which he had in mind with the United States, and I remembered how on Contadora he had said that 1977 was the year when his patience would be exhausted. Confrontation meant war – a war between a tiny republic with less than 2,000,000 inhabitants and the United States with more than 200,000,000.

Torrijos, I had begun to realize, was a romantic, but in most Panamanians I was soon to find that romanticism was balanced by a streak of cynical wisdom which you can detect in their popular songs – they are far less sentimental than ours – for example, 'Your love is a yesterday's newspaper', and you can read cynicism even in some of the slogans on the beautifully painted buses – 'Don't go and get dressed up, because you are not going with me.' The General may have felt self-destructive, but he had estimated his chances realistically.

'We could hold Panama City for forty-eight hours,' he told me. 'As for the Canal, it is easy to sabotage. Blow a hole in the

54

Gatún Dam and the Canal will drain into the Atlantic. It would take only a few days to mend the dam, but it would take three years of rain to fill the Canal. During that time it would be guerrilla war; the central *cordilleras* rise to 3,000 metres and extend to the Costa Rican frontier on one side of the Zone and the dense Darién jungle, almost as unknown as in the days of Balboa, stretches on the other side to the Colombian border, crossed only by smugglers' paths. Here we could hold out for two years – long enough to rouse the conscience of the world and public opinion in the States. And don't forget – for the first time since the Civil War American civilians would be in the firing line. There are 40,000 of them in the Zone, apart from the 10,000 troops.'

There were areas of jungle in the Zone itself where the Americans were training their own special troops, as well as troops from other Latin American states, in guerrilla warfare, but he regarded this training, from personal experience, with some contempt. Recently when the Americans were holding jungle manoeuvres inside the Zone they were surprised to encounter a patrol of the Wild Pigs who had penetrated the Zone unobserved because, as their officer explained with courtesy, something had gone wrong with his compass. The General added, 'I know the Pentagon advised Carter that they would need 100,000 men, not 10,000, to defend the Canal properly.'

Our conversation was interrupted by the noise of the General's small jet plane arriving from Venezuela. He had sent it off that morning with a letter to the President and it was returning with the President's reply. (The only support on which the General could count in South America during his negotiations with the United States was from Venezuela, Colombia and Peru.) Communications were much as they had been in the seventeenth century – by messenger; a jet plane had taken the place of a horse. As the American Zone was packed with electronic equipment any telephone call could be tapped and a telegraphic code could be broken in a matter of hours.

General Torrijos read the letter from the President of

Venezuela and afterwards the conversation took a completely different turn. I had the impression that what came now was the real reason why he wanted me to stay – not me in particular perhaps, but any listener who would understand his emotion. He said, 'Yesterday a most important thing happened.'

I wondered, 'Is he going to disclose some secret message from old Mr Bunker – or from those international characters whom Mr Drummond's supporters called Gerry and Henry?'

He went on, 'Yesterday I had been married twenty-five years, but when I married – I was only a young lieutenant – my father-in-law, who is a Jewish business man living in New York, swore that he would never speak to his daughter again. It has been very hard for my wife all these years, for she loves her father dearly. A few days ago I asked General Dayan to inter-cede for me in New York. My father-in-law wouldn't even listen to Dayan. Panama had voted at the United Nations in support of Israel over the Entebbe affair. We were the only state in Latin America to do so, and afterwards the Israelis were grateful and they offered me all sorts of help, but I told them that I had asked Dayan for the only thing I needed and he couldn't help me. Then suddenly, yesterday, my father-in-law telephoned from New York and asked to speak to my wife. Today she has gone off to see him – after twenty-five years. I said to the old man on the telephone that he had a wonderful daughter and that I owed everything to her.'

What he had told me was the more moving because he would have known that by this time I would be aware he was not the kind of man to be sexually faithful to one woman. But he was a man who had a deep loyalty to the past, and was faithful above all to friendship.

10

Chuchu and I had planned to fly off to the island of Taboga for a rest after our travels, but it was not to be. The General wanted me back at Rio Hato the next day to go with him to a meeting of farmers and rural representatives. It was to be an example for me of how his type of democracy worked.

We took a small military plane and flew out to sea, making a wide sweep before returning to the coast. The General said, 'You can tell today that we have a young pilot – inexperienced – because he is flying over the sea. The older ones hug the land. Because it's safer in a small plane. By reason of the sharks down there. Sometimes when I know that my pilot will refuse to take me by some route because of the weather, I ask for a young one who won't know better.'

It was obvious that he was enjoying the slight risk involved of the descent into a shark-ridden sea. Had he demanded a young pilot on the day of his death, I wonder five years later?

I asked him on the plane, I don't know for what reason, when it was during the day that he was liable to feel the most discouraged (he seemed to like such personal questions as though he felt in them the approach of a nearer friendship). He replied immediately, 'At night when I go to bed. But when the sun rises I feel cheerful.'

If I was getting to know the General a little more at every meeting it was by his own wish. It was as though he had become bored and haunted by his public image and he wanted above all to be a private person who could talk to a friend, saying this and that without any forethought.

It was a group of yucca farmers whom we were now going to meet and listen to their complaints. After we landed, on the road to the village, he told me that he had decided to grant their demand for a rise from one dollar twenty-five cents to one dollar seventy-five cents a box. 'This yucca centre has been a mistake – our mistake, not theirs. Anyway, I want to redistribute money, more to the country and less to the towns.' All the same, he added, he would keep the peasants guessing for a while – for his amusement and theirs.

The meeting was in the open and before me I saw arranged the same faces, in the same funny hats, with the same protruding pie-dog ears, as the friends of the sandal-maker. Indeed, I am convinced that one of them was a peasant whom I had met that day at Ocú because he continually caught my eye and winked at me. Many of them had gold teeth and quite a number gold rings – Columbus perhaps would have taken it for a sign that Eldorado was not far away. They all tried to talk at once and to look fierce and determined, and the General, I could see, was thoroughly enjoying himself.

He began, 'We'll take the easy points first and we'll leave the difficult yucca question to the last.' It was a clever way of getting through things rapidly, for the peasants were only interested in the yucca, so that there was no disputing his other decisions. There was to be a new canal bridge, he promised, to ease the traffic across the Zone on the Bridge of the Americas; the location of a lime processing plant was left for later consideration; the plan for a mixed enterprise (sixty per cent private) for raising cattle was also left for another occasion. His audience were all glad to leave everything for another occasion except the yucca, including a question of salt refining and the use of salt in road construction.

Finally, with a stir of excited interest, came the price of yucca. The government, the General said, had been too ambitious in the encouragement of yucca. There had been many errors. All the same he doubted whether it was possible for him to raise the price. Who was going to provide the money? It would have to come out of the pocket of somebody.

The government engineer tried to speak. The General interrupted, saying it was the farmers he had come to hear.

He spoke again about the difficulties in putting up the price – exports mustn't be endangered. Perhaps a rise of twenty cents . . . ? And he began to haggle over the cents. All the same there was amusement in his eyes. He was teasing them.

The peasants soon began to see what he was up to, and now they argued with half smiles and disputed with cracks of humour, till suddenly the General gave way. Then there was laughter and clapping. They had got the price which they had asked for. This was important, but above all the rest they had had a lot of fun. The meeting broke up gaily.

What followed was not so amusing – a dull lunch at a landowner's house with a lot of boring women who clustered around the General where he lay in his inevitable hammock and we were served with almost uneatable pieces of pork and quite uneatable yucca (which I now realized was what I called cassava) with only a choice of water or Pepsi to drink. Oh, for a whisky or a glass of rum, but this was not a Sunday. Even the General drank water. I was at my wits' end until Chuchu, who was standing guard at the door, caught my eye and winked. I went outside. He had found me a drink in a room out of sight of the party.

After the plane had deposited the General at Rio Hato Chuchu and I drove back to Panama. We stopped at the Haunted House and had a drink in the bar next door, for Chuchu seemed in my company to be developing the European habit of drinking all days of the week.

I had told the General about our first visit, and he remembered having heard of the ghost even as a child. It was said to be that of a headless white woman. The owner must be nearly eighty by now, so when the haunting began he was a man in his thirties. I became convinced that he had killed the woman in his house, her screams had been heard, and so the story of the haunting was invented. She was probably buried under the floor. I suggested to the General that he hold an exercise by the Wild Pigs. They would break into the house after a notional siege and perhaps do a bit of digging. But the General didn't approve the idea. Any search, he said, would have to be legal.

Chuchu and I took another prowl around. We asked the barman if he had seen the owner. Oh yes, he had mentioned our visit, but there was nothing to be done without speaking to him. He was always there on a Sunday. Well, we would return the next Sunday, we said.

In Panama City Chuchu suggested that he ask for dinner 'the rich woman' (so it was that he always described her to distinguish her from all the others, but I don't think she was very wealthy). He had planned to spend the night with her anyway – in a hotel because of the child. She would have to get up at six to go home. What about the girl he was living with at the moment, I asked?

Oh, she was all right. She made no demands on him. Women, Chuchu admitted, seemed to like him. 'You are a good lover?' Oh, it wasn't exactly that, he said. He wasn't concerned with sexual positions and that sort of nonsense, nor did he think that women were really interested in such unimportant details. What they liked in him, he believed, was the tenderness which he always showed them after making love. This particular 'wife', as he called her, was beautiful.

We each drank three rum punches at the excellent bar of the Señorial and they were made for us by an attractive young woman called Flor. She was obviously fond of Chuchu, but he was strangely reluctant to court her ('She's a good woman. The affair might turn too serious'). Afterwards we went off to meet the poet. Chuchu was already a little drunk.

He became a good deal more drunk over dinner, continually demanding that I admire the beauty of his friend. She was certainly a good-looking and intelligent woman in her late forties or early fifties, but it was difficult to carry on a conversation when every few moments Chuchu would say, 'Look at her, Graham, look at her, isn't she lovely?' She showed, I thought, great patience. He drove me rather erratically back to the hotel, and then they went away together. It seemed to me that his chances of a satisfactory night with her were small.

How wrong I was. He turned up next day to meet me, very happy and still a little drunk. (He had had half a bottle of wine for his breakfast before she left him at six.) It was a 'wonderful night', he said. I told him that I was surprised after the way he had treated her at dinner.

'What do you mean?'

'You kept on telling me to look at her and see how beautiful she was. It was the only thing you did say.'

'You don't understand, Graham,' he replied. 'She has reached the age when she needs reassurance.'

He was indeed something better than a professor of Marxist philosophy and of mathematics and a sergeant in the security guard – he was a good and a kind man with a human wisdom much greater than my own. I think my deep affection for him began that day, when he was too drunk to drive with safety. He broke through the lights and ran into a parked car before we landed at a bookshop kept by a Greek war hero. 'We have to invite him to your party on Friday,' he said.

'*My* party?'

It appeared that the General and Chuchu had decided between them that I was to be the host at a party. The drinks would be provided by the National Guard, and the party would be held at the house of an old Panamanian writer, Rogelio Sinan. The General wouldn't be able to attend as he was busy with the Refrigerator, old Mr Bunker, and his American delegation. 'We'll invite the Cubans,' Chuchu said (he had quite forgiven them for the defective Russian pistol), 'but we will not invite Señor V.' There was an American, he warned me, who would certainly turn up whether he was invited or not – a writer called Koster who lived in Panama City and was supposed to be a CIA agent. He had asked Chuchu about me. 'What's the old goat doing here?' he had enquired. I looked forward to meeting him.

11

The next day the General lent us an army helicopter which landed us after lunch on the beach of Taboga in front of the little hotel there. They would come to fetch us again for the party in Panama City two days later. The island was very small, but included a village and a jungle. Somewhere buried in the jungle – but we couldn't find the path – was an English cemetery; its inhabitants could now be regarded as buried twice over. Years ago, about the time when Panama had joined Colombia to become a nation, there had been a British commercial establishment on the island, perhaps in connexion with de Lesseps's Canal project. Gauguin had visited the island twice, but was disappointed on his second visit because he found the peace had been disturbed by a branch of the Canal company. Now peace had returned again.

Chuchu and I bathed with caution in the surf, for there were sharks, though we were assured that for some mysterious reason they confined themselves to the waters around the next island, visible only too clearly about a mile away. We had sandwiches and beer and walked in the village. In the evening the one sea bus arrived carrying the islanders who worked on the mainland. The peace of the place without cars was so deep that it was like a tune running in the head. In the passage outside my room there was a polite notice with an English translation: 'If you expect visits of the opposite sex, please receive them in the public areas.' It seemed an oddly puritanical request for Panama. Chuchu and I had a pin-table tournament, but I don't remember which of us won. Then I went to bed and dreamt – in reaction from all this peace – that I received a disquieting telegram from home.

Next day I woke from my dream to the same tune of peace, peace, peace, and we did exactly the same things. We bathed, we breakfasted, we walked in the village, we bathed again. It was as though we had been living for many quiet months on the island. But one false note was struck. Chuchu was called out of the sea by a telephone call from Señor V. He wasn't, thank God, joining us as I feared, but he had taken over all the arrangements for the party to which we had not intended even to invite him. That evening, I remember, the light was particularly beautiful – we could forget Señor V. The white hazy towers of Panama City shimmering ten miles away across the sea were like an engraving of paradise by John Martin.

In bed I reread *Heart of Darkness* as I had done last in 1958 in the Congo. My novel, so I believed, was taking form in my head, hope was reborn, and I thought that I had found in Conrad an epigraph for *On the Way Back*. But now when I reopen Conrad's story at the page which I had marked, the sentences seem more suitable to the book I am writing now:

It seems I am trying to tell you a dream – making a vain attempt, because no relation of a dream can convey the dream's sensation, that commingling of absurdity, surprise, and bewilderment and a tremor of struggling revolt, that notion of being captured by the incredible . . .

In the peace of Taboga I felt captivated by Panama, by the struggle with the United States, by the peasants barking like dogs, by Chuchu's strange wisdom and complicated sex life, by the drumbeats in the slums of El Chorillo, by the General's dreams of death, and as for revolt, I was to feel that too at moments in the years that followed – the desire to be back in Europe with the personal, understandable problems there.

Next morning I began trying to compose in my diary the first sentences of the novel, describing how a young French woman journalist was engaged by a fashionable Paris left-wing editor to go to Panama to interview the General. They proved in fact not to be the first sentences in the chapter which I was finally to write and then abandon:

He was tall and lean and he would have had an air of almost overpowering distinction if his grey hair had not been quite so well waved over his ears, which were again of the right masculine size. She would perhaps have taken him for a diplomat if she had not known him to be the editor of a very distinguished weekly which she seldom read, being out of sympathy with its modish tendency towards left-wing politics. Many men come alive only in their eyes: his eyes were dead, and it was only in the gestures of his elegant carcase that he lived.

I admit that I had a certain editor in mind whom I had only met once in a Lisbon bar, and, for the first time as a novelist, I was trying mistakenly to use real characters – the General, Chuchu, even this editor – in my fiction. They had emerged from life and not from the unconscious and for that reason they stood motionless like statues in my mind – they couldn't develop, they were incapable of the unexpected word or action – they were real people and they could have no life independent of me in the imagination.

12

The helicopter landed with military punctuality on the beach to fetch us and back in Panama City I took a long siesta to prepare for this odd party of which I was to be the host, host to a lot of strangers chosen by Chuchu and Señor V. The Greek bookseller was the only one I would even know by sight.

On the invitation cards the party was timed for eight till ten. Chuchu and I arrived punctually and so did many of the guests, but not the drinks. Time passed very slowly without them. The party stagnated. A lot of photographs were taken of disconsolate groups. Chuchu was looking tired. He told me he had spent the afternoon with a prostitute. The party grew larger and larger, but there were still no drinks, and the hypocrisy of such parties came bitterly home to me. Nobody goes to a party to meet anyone: everybody is there for free drinks. There were no drinks and I was supposed to be the host.

I took a strong dislike to the Cuban Attaché for Political Affairs who seemed to regard me with deep suspicion after I told him that I had been three times to Cuba since the revolution and had known the country in the days of Batista. Luckily I was saved from him by a very nice young Cuban press officer. Chuchu slipped away (in search of the drinks, he had explained to me), and after what seemed a long time he returned triumphantly with a lorry load of them. Apparently he had given the wrong address to the National Guard.

The party quickly cheered up. The leading Communist in Panama proved very friendly. He told me how his party supported the General's policy of 'prudence'. A young black architect agreed with me about the stupidity of high-rise apartments in the poor quarter of El Chorillo – even the slum houses of Hollywood were to be preferred, he said. I was confused by his reference to Hollywood which I associated with film stars rather than with slums. 'The people in Hollywood are attached to their houses,' he told me. 'The conditions are terrible, but all the same they are homes.' I realized tardily that Hollywood must be the name given to a very poor part of the city.

Chuchu nudged me. 'There's Koster.'

The novelist – or CIA agent – was circulating assiduously, drawing ever nearer, except when he made a sideways dash to refill his glass. The National Guard had done us well and I was feeling a little tipsy myself by this time. Koster reached me and held out his hand.

'Koster,' he said.

'The old goat,' I introduced myself.

'What do you mean?'

'Chuchu told me that you wanted to know what the old goat was doing here.'

'I never said such a thing.'

He moved quickly away to hide himself among the other guests and according to Chuchu he spread a rather strange story that I was a well-known homosexual. Are goats homosexual?

Ten o'clock was long past: the drinks were inexhaustible: and at midnight guests were still arriving. Feeling a discourteous host, I slunk away with Chuchu and his companion, the somewhat haggard woman whom Chuchu fancied, the refugee from Argentina and the dictatorship of Videla. There were many such refugees in Panama City and there was a special flat for their use, known locally as the Pigeon House, for when they had found work or entry into another country they flew away. Chuchu supported them out of the General's private account.

Chuchu had confided to me over the drinks that the only wife he had ever really loved (she was a legal wife, too) was arriving next day from the States where she lived with her new husband, a professor, to see her mother and she was bringing with her Chuchu's two children whom he had not seen for seven years. Her husband was following her in a few days, but I could tell that Chuchu all the same had hopes, and it was obvious that the Argentinian woman was of little importance to him for the time being.

The day after the party one of my ambitions was fulfilled. Chuchu took me to Portobelo. It wasn't Nombre de Dios, which I was not to see for another two years, but it was in Portobelo Bay that Drake's body was buried. An American officer was aiding the Panamanians in what proved an unsuccessful search there for his coffin.

Portobelo is fantastically beautiful. Little seems altered since Drake's day when the town stood at the end of the gold route from Panama City. Here is still the treasure house where the gold awaited shipment to Spain, the three forts guarding the town, the ramparts which are lined now with vultures: vultures too were sitting on and around the cross of the cathedral. From the door of the cathedral one could see nothing of the village, only the jungle descending like a curtain, dark and impenetrable, to within fifty yards of the door. There seemed little room among the stone ruins even for the small population of two thousand. The statue of a black Christ presided over the altar. It had been shipwrecked on the way to the Viceroy of Peru and salvaged by the Indians.

Back in Panama City I lay down for a siesta, but it was not to be. Chuchu woke me to say that the General wanted us to come over to Rory González's house – Mr Bunker and the Americans had left after only a few days on Contadora island and the General was celebrating.

It was the first time that we had a real drinking party together. At lunch he would drink water, and only when he had realized my European desire for a real drink did he concede me a glass of rum. This evening Black Label was already flowing when I arrived with Chuchu at five and it continued to flow till ten when I left. Señor V was there. He was already on his way to being well stoned, so that he was no menace now to my independence and it proved to be the last time I saw the poor

66

man alive. The young Panamanian Ambassador to the United States was there too, and of course Rory González.

The General, relieved from the tedium of negotiations, was happy and confiding. He showed me photographs of his wife with the father whom she had recovered. They looked as happy as the General. He joked about the beautiful Colombian singer he had flown to Bogotá to see. *'You* saw her,' he said, 'but I measured her.' All the same he told me, perhaps from chivalry for he was a chivalrous man, that he had been disappointed, nothing had happened, she wouldn't even get into his plane.

'We are celebrating the end of Panama's number one bachelor,' he told me. 'Rory's getting married on December twenty-seven.' He himself had been married when he was twenty-three. He regretted nothing, he said, though there had been troubles. His young wife had discovered a *cache* of his love letters. 'She wasn't hysterical,' he said, 'she was historical.' He had found himself virtually imprisoned in his home and had to appeal to Rory to come and rescue him.

Black Label made the hours spin past. It was nearly nine o'clock and Chuchu whispered urgently to me. He must be off to the airport to meet his ex-wife and his children. 'Please come with me, Graham,' he pleaded. But I was happy and I wouldn't go.

'Then please lend me your dark glasses.'

'Whatever for? It's pitch black outside.'

'To hide my tears,' he said.

The General spoke of the banana war some years back between the United Fruit Company and the banana-producing states. One by one they had made terms with the company until only Panama held out. 'The company said they were prepared to offer me three million dollars. If they had offered me two Miss Universes, who knows . . .'

At ten I could drink no more and the General had disappeared. Rory said he would send me home in his car, since Chuchu had not returned. I asked him to thank the General for me. He said, 'I think he's with a girl.' Señor V was tipped into the rear seat. He was completely sozzled and I couldn't understand a word he said on his way to the hotel.

My sense of happiness stayed with me all the way to bed. Panama had not yet got a currency of its own – dollars were the only tender, but soon the General had promised a Panama coinage . . . when once the Canal situation had been solved . . . Drowsing in my bed, I thought of a design for the future Panama coin. Might it not be suitably stamped on one side with the image of the General and on the other with the image of Chuchu, the images of two romantics who trusted each other more than they did any woman or politician or intellectual?

13

Chuchu turned up at my hotel with the two attractive and intelligent children he had made with the woman he most loved. On a later occasion, after yet another marriage and another child, he remarked to me of her with regret, 'Ah, *she* wasn't a clean woman.' I think he meant only that she had not been fussy about order and propriety. She had not been 'wifely'.

Once again we tried to get a plane to Bocas del Toro, the island which had become an obsession with me almost as strong as the village of Nombre de Dios, and once again luckily we failed. So instead we drove the children along the interrupted Inter-American highway towards Colombia, towards the great empty space coloured green on the map which marks the thick uncleared jungle of Darién, the reserve of uncountable Indians. There were those (among them Japanese engineers) who wanted to build a new canal through the jungle which would be cleared with the help of nuclear devices, but the General was firmly opposed to the idea. 'We don't know how many thousands of Indians would be killed or displaced.'

On the edge of this great reserve the Bayano Dam had been constructed with the help of the Yugoslavs. We reached it after having lunched at an army post for recruits – it was Sunday and a visiting day for their families and I was reminded of my English school on Founder's Day with proud mothers and embarrassed boys.

The dam had caused the displacement of at least one Indian village, which now lay below the water. We went up to see the new village which had taken its place and in the assembly hut we were greeted by the chief, an old man of immense dignity who wore two feathers in his hat and a length of green material slung over one shoulder. A number of villagers sat on the floor and listened in silence while an interpreter voiced the chief's complaints against the government. They were not going to let the opportunity of our visit pass them by.

The government had not kept its promises, we were told – the payment which had been guaranteed them for their re-settlement was three months in arrears; they had been moved to the new village too late for planting: they were short of sugar and grain: the wild animals which used to provide them with food had been driven away by the work on the dam and all the fish in the river had been killed. If they were to appeal to the General, the appeal would have to be co-ordinated through all the Indian chiefs, and the man who was likely to be chosen as their representative was a bad one who did nothing at all to help his people. We promised the chief that we would speak directly to the General and he believed us – though perhaps with a certain scepticism.

Chuchu's children listened with great gravity. It must have seemed to them a very long way from their home in the United States and from their stepfather on the campus. Chuchu was a professor too, but in his army uniform and his sergeant's stripes he must have seemed very different from the professors whom they were accustomed to meet in the United States. Chuchu cleverly brought his son out. 'Tell me a thought,' he would say to him, and again, 'Give me a thought about that,' and his son promptly responded with little aphorisms.

Later back in Panama City Chuchu and I went unwillingly to the Holiday Inn because it happened to be close by in order to drink three rum punches each – which as we feared proved to be poor ones – and discuss plans for the next day. We would take an army helicopter to one of the San Blas Islands in the Atlantic where the lobsters were good, according to Chuchu, and the Cuna Indians lived an independent life. Then we went on to the Marisco for dinner and Chuchu found that he had forgotten his spectacles and went to find them – he had in fact forgotten more than his spectacles, for he returned with 'the little girl' whom he hadn't the heart to leave. She was charming and not nearly so simple as he made out.

14

In Panama City nothing ever happened as we had planned. Instead of taking the helicopter to the San Blas Islands we went shopping because the General wanted us to sit with him at Rory's while he scrambled through his lunch (he hated to be alone while he ate). I thought I would try to change his taste in whisky. I bought a bottle of Irish whiskey (I wanted to teach him how to make Irish coffee and I had learned that he did not even know that Ireland produced whiskey) and a bottle of Glenfiddich to challenge his favourite Black Label. I also gave him one of the treasures which I kept in my pocket book – a fake dollar note with the reverse printed with propaganda against the Vietnam war. This pleased him more than the whisky, for he continued to be faithful to Black Label till the end. They were to be farewell presents, for next day my KLM plane would be taking off for Amsterdam.

We told him of the Indian complaints at Bayano and he promised that they would be attended to and he gave Chuchu's notes to his secretary. Then we talked at random while the simple meal seemed to be swallowed almost untasted with the help of water – Sunday was over. We talked of dreams – he seldom remembered them and those he remembered were disturbing like that of his dead father – of women ('When one is

young one eats anything but now one distinguishes'), of premonitions, from which he often suffered. His premonitions
were usually of his own death by violence. I told him how
appalling I found the Walt Disney figures on the roads of the
Republic to which the names of villages and towns were
attached. 'Next time the students want to demonstrate against
the States, can't you tell them to burn all those Donald Ducks?'
Alas, my suggestion was never taken up. They are still there.

As we talked, the solitary budgerigar watched us from its cage.
'It will never sing,' I said to Torrijos, 'without a companion.'

'Oh yes, it will,' he said. He went into the next room and
fetched a little cassette. He had recorded the song of a budgerigar and he played it to the solitary bird which burst into
song in reply. How could one fail, I thought, to like this man?

That evening Chuchu and I went to the open-air restaurant,
the Panama, where the Pacific lay like a dark lawn in front and
the stars seemed brighter and nearer than they ever were at
home. We were to meet his ex-wife and their children, and
Chuchu, while we waited, described her to me as the most
beautiful woman I had probably ever seen. He knew he would
feel so sad at parting from her when dinner was over that he
had arranged for his comfort a rendezvous at half-past ten with
a prostitute at a certain street corner – 'the little girl' at home
would be quite incapable of soothing his unhappiness.

Chuchu's ex-wife arrived. She was good-looking, intelligent,
and certainly a very nice woman, but I found her hardly the
equal of Chuchu's dream. She had brought with her (I think it
may have been as a barrier against Chuchu's attentions) a pretty
young woman doctor who bristled with suspicion. Chuchu had
put on his best uniform: he had combed his unruly hair and
now he set out to seduce his thirteen-year-old daughter. Like
Chuchu she was a romantic – in a few years' time a friend of
mine met her in Nicaragua, wearing khaki with a revolver on
her hip.

All through dinner Chuchu talked of his loneliness here in
Panama: quite forgotten were the rich woman and his baby,

'the little girl' waiting at home, the prostitute by this time on her way to the rendezvous. 'When you go back to the States,' he implored his ex-wife, 'at least leave me my daughter.' His daughter held his hand and wept for the lonely man at her side – he wasn't the professor that night, he was a soldier. Her young brother was of tougher material and he proudly produced a 'thought' as his father had taught him. 'He can't be lonely with the whole world in his mind.' The doctor watched Chuchu's performance cynically and the girl cried and cried.

I was furious with Chuchu and I berated him as he drove me back to the hotel. 'You had no right,' I told him, 'to upset your daughter like that with stories of your loneliness. Loneliness! What sort of loneliness?'

'But I am lonely,' he said. He stopped the car at a corner and looked up and down the road. 'She's gone,' he said, 'we are nearly an hour late.'

Next day I had my last meal with Chuchu at the Marisco – a farewell to Panama – a meal given us free by the Basque owner. It was very light and elegant, consisting only of the cheeks of fish in oil and a Chilean wine chosen from a non-Pinochet year.

I never thought I would see Chuchu or the General or Panama again, but I was haunted still by the novel I was never to write and in the months that followed I wrote down snatches of dialogue – though not the dialogue I had heard spoken.

'You judge us,' the General was saying not to me but to the woman reporter of *On the Way Back*. 'You call us Latin Americans because you won't look deep enough inside yourselves – where you would find us too.

'Who was the first Latin American? Cortés – not Columbus. Columbus stayed on his boat in Portobelo Bay and wouldn't land. He was old, like Europe.'

But there was one genuine line of the General's dialogue which haunted me still by its mystery. What had he meant when he said, 'You and I are both self-destructive'? It was like a friend speaking who knew me better than I knew myself.

PART II

1977

1

The novel *On the Way Back* nagged at me night and day on my return to France. Those characters which I had so mistakenly drawn from life wouldn't let me rest. I would constantly remember Chuchu's boast, 'I'm never going to die'; his complex theology – 'I believe in the Devil. I don't believe in God,' and the way that he would prove the existence of the Devil by pushing at a swing door in the wrong direction. The General and Chuchu went on living, far away in Panama, and they refused to become characters in my novel. And Panama – so much of the little country had still been left unseen and it seemed highly unlikely that I would ever be able to return for a second visit. I hadn't got as far as Columbus to the undesirable island of Bocas del Toro; Nombre de Dios was a name only in a pageant and a poem; we had failed to penetrate the Haunted House. News came to me, I think from my friend Diederich, that Señor V, poor man, was dead of a heart attack. Had that last Black Label party been too much for him? In the novel, which I began to despair of ever writing, it was essential that he should remain alive, for his role was an important one. After Chuchu's death in his bombed car – at David? – the General had to send Señor V to fetch the girl back by helicopter to Panama City, and it was in his unsympathetic company that she would find herself being flown over all the places which she and Chuchu had planned to visit 'on the way back'.

I put the first two pages of the doomed book down on paper in the months that followed. Marie-Claire, the French journalist, arrived as I had done on that first occasion to see the General.

She found herself surrounded in the small courtyard of a white suburban villa with half-Indian faces. The men all carried revolvers on their belts and one had a walkie-talkie which he kept pressed closely to his ear as though he were waiting with the intensity of a priest for one of his Indian gods to proclaim something. The men are as strange to me, she thought, as the Indians must have seemed to Columbus five centuries ago. The camouflage of their uniforms was like painted designs on naked skin.

I had not got much further with the book when one night at bedtime my telephone rang in Antibes. It was the voice of Chuchu speaking from Panama. 'When are you coming?'

'What do you mean?'

'The General wants to know when you are coming.'

'But . . .'

'Your ticket is waiting for you at KLM.'

So after all, I thought with a certain happiness, I am going to see Panama once more.

On this occasion I flew from Paris to Amsterdam, so as to catch the KLM flight, and next morning I was drinking Bols once again over the Caribbean. In my diary I noted: '21 August. Towering cloud formations above Trinidad. Lovely mountainous coast of Colombia and then the dense Darién jungle. Chuchu met me at airport.'

It was as though I had never been away. Life without any difficulty began to change to the Panama rhythm. A siesta, bad planter's punches with Chuchu at the Holiday Inn, back for my whisky at the hotel, a good dinner from the Basque *patron* at the Marisco. However, there were some important changes and Chuchu brought me up to date. His own life had not stood still. Chuchu's beloved ex-wife had left her American husband, but she had written to Chuchu saying she wouldn't return to him (rather, I think, to his relief) because when she was with him she didn't feel free. He said, 'She's trying to be a hundred per cent something, when what she really wants is to be fifty per cent – half-free, half-intelligent, half . . .' He was still consorting with the Argentinian refugee, but now she would some-times hit him out of jealousy.

And the General? How was the General? He was unhappy, Chuchu told me, about the terms of the Canal Treaty to which he had finally agreed, he was sleeping badly and he was not even drinking at weekends – a bad sign. Chuchu was very much in favour of getting the students to demonstrate against the Zone before the American Senate could meet to consider the Treaty, just to show them that Panama was not ready to accept any changes which they might choose to make. But the big question in his mind was whether the General was not moving perhaps a little towards the right.

I had published an article in the *New York Review of Books* on 'The Country with Five Frontiers' in which I had written that some of the senior officers in the National Guard had special privileges, in the way of housing for example, because, as the General had said to me, 'If I don't pay them, the CIA will,' and I had described Colonel Flores as he sat chewing his gum at the meeting in El Chorillo. Chuchu had translated my article for a Panamanian paper, and he had asked the General whether he perhaps should leave out my reference to the National Guard officers. 'No. You don't alter a word of his,' the General had replied. So much then for my future relationship with the Chief of Staff. I hoped that there would be no *coup d'état* while I was in Panama.

Chuchu put the problem to me in this way: 'Of course there is corruption among a few of the senior officers. You know the story of the man who was trying to clean his lavatory with one of those rubber squeegees and it didn't work. A man said to him, "You'll never clear it that way. You have to put your hands in the shit and pull it out." The General has got to put his hands in the shit.'

The next day the General sent his plane to fetch the two of us to his house at Farallón on the Pacific coast for lunch. 'Pack a handbag,' Chuchu warned me. 'I have an idea we won't be returning to the city today.'

77

Chuchu was right. A helicopter was waiting by the house and we left our bags in it.

I was surprised, after what Chuchu had told me, to find how relaxed, young, and even happy Torrijos seemed – he greeted me by my Christian name and an embrace, so that I followed suit, and he became Omar to me from that moment on. He told me that he had liked my article. He said, 'You describe me as a real person and not a computer.' It was true, he went on, that the negotiations over the Treaty had been very hard and exhausting. The Americans had begun them with the idea of not surrendering anything. Now the final words had been spoken and the issue lay in the lap of the gods – or of the Senate. Some nights ago he had had a very vivid dream. The guerrilla war, which in a way he desired, had begun. He was in the jungle and he found himself without his boots. He felt an awful humiliation, for he would be captured right at the start of a war only because he had no boots.

After lunch the helicopter's engine was turned on, but the General led the way to a car and took the wheel. The helicopter was left empty except for our bags. The last-minute change was for security – a measure against some violent end, which I think now was always in his mind. There were five of us in the car, the General, myself, Chuchu, the General's secretary and a young girl friend with a pretty face which contained a hint of Chinese blood. She seemed at that first meeting a little pretentious and a would-be intellectual – she was studying sociology in the States, a subject which thrives on banalities and abstract jargon – but I was quite wrong about her. She had intelligence and courage, tenderness and loyalty, and she was good for Omar.

Apparently we were going to Santiago for the night and next day the helicopter would join us and take us to David and then to a Panamanian banana plantation – the only one of any size owned by the Republic. It was surrounded by American-owned plantations.

Santiago was the General's birthplace. He told me as he

drove how at sixteen he tried to run away from home with a girl and he had stolen his elder brother's car. 'I was lucky,' he said. 'The police stopped me as we were leaving Santiago. I sometimes see the girl now in the street. She is a woman who has become enormously fat.'

At the edge of Santiago we halted at the house of a lorry owner, an old friend of Omar's. The man had recently discovered some magnificent gold necklaces in a tomb which he had secretly excavated. He claimed that they were four thousand years old, and the General advised him to keep them hidden until he could arrange for the government to pay him a fair price. Then we drove on into Santiago, and he pointed out the little wooden house of his father, the school-teacher, and of his grandfather. He felt happy and at ease in this small home town. There was no sense of 'showing off'.

We went to the house of a garage mechanic with whom he had been at school, and we sat outside in rocking chairs while neighbours gathered and rocked with us and drank whisky which Omar had unobtrusively provided. Before we arrived he told me how on a former visit he had abused this friend for drunkenness and the man replied, 'It's because I wouldn't meet you at the airport. I'm no arse licker, and which of us two is happier? I can drink all day if I want to and nobody cares.' At one moment, when his friend was out of earshot, Omar remarked to me, 'If I had stayed here, my horizon would have been no wider than this porch,' but there was a note of apology in his voice, as if he had a sense of guilt because of his escape.

After the gossip about the past, the conversation turned inevitably to the Treaty. The General's disappointment with the terms was not shared by his friend the garage mechanic.

Presently a schoolmistress arrived with some of her senior girls, and the General talked to them, not down to them. I noted in my diary that night:

I've never known him to talk down to anyone – even to a child of five. With peasants he jokes coarsely, but so he sometimes does with us. I

79

asked the oldest schoolgirl, a tall girl of around seventeen, what should be done if the Treaty were not ratified and she said without hesitation, 'Anything is better than blood again in the streets.'

We talked of more frivolous things after dinner. Omar showed no signs of having given up drink, although it was a Monday and not a weekend. The conversation became sexual. I don't remember now what aspect of a woman's feelings or preferences I touched on, but I remember how strongly Omar disagreed with me. His young mistress came to my support and the General complained with a smile, 'You are upsetting my domestic peace.' It was a happy, tipsy evening untroubled by doubts of the Treaty.

2

After breakfast the General received two visitors from the town, a young man and his mother. He listened with kindness and patience to their long-drawn-out story. It was of a sad and common kind; the woman's husband had recently died and the boy was unemployed. It proved easier to solve their problems than those of Mr Bunker. Omar wrote them two notes – one to the municipality telling them to lower the mother's rent and one to the manager of a sugar-cane factory ordering him to give the boy employment. To me it seemed that the General was practising a direct form of democracy, though the General's enemies would have called him a populist, a word which is now commonly misemployed and used as a sneer. (My Oxford Dictionary published in 1969 defines it in two senses: 'Adherent of US political party aiming at public control of railways etc.,' or 'Adherent of Russian political party advocating collectivism.')

By this time the helicopter had arrived with our bags and we left the car behind and flew on to David, and then after a short stop we went in search of the very elusive banana plantation. Surrounded as it was by the plantations owned by United Brands (a title by which the United Fruit Company has tried to escape from its unsavoury past), it was difficult to distinguish one from another at a thousand feet, with the result that we made two landings on American plantations.

At the first Omar pretended that he had landed there on purpose and demanded the way to the school, where he was greeted with some awe by the master and with excitement by the pupils. He talked a little to the children and looked at their schoolbooks. Peasants gathered in the doorway. I asked one of them what should be done if the Treaty were not ratified. 'Fight, of course,' he said and his companion grunted approval. Apparently in this village on an American estate the people had struggled for a long time in vain to get a school established. Anyone who agitated for the school was regarded by the American company as a Communist and many were sent to prison in the States quite illegally, for the plantation was not in the Zone. Once a captain of police was ordered to beat up the villagers, but he refused. They had their school now, but the spirit of belligerence remained.

Here some intelligent questions were asked the General about the future, when, by the terms of the Treaty, a large part of the American Zone would be returned immediately to Panama, with the exception of the military bases. No private building would be allowed, the General assured them. That part of the Zone which adjoined the poorest quarter of Panama City, known satirically as Hollywood, would become a public park. He had plans too for an orphanage . . . He said, 'We are not going to exchange white landlords for coffee-coloured ones.' He welcomed direct questions from his own people. It was only from journalists he resented them. I remembered his reply to a journalist who asked him if he were a Marxist: 'An interview is not a confessional. I don't have to tell you my thoughts. Shall I ask you if you are a pederast?' Well, if he was a populist, I thought, I would prefer populism in Panama to Marxism or conservatism or liberalism.

Back we went to the helicopter and down again on to another plantation, which proved again to be American. This time the

General despaired of finding the way by helicopter and he telephoned for a car. It was very hot and we waited a long time and when the car came Chuchu was knocked down by the swarm of children rushing at the General, determined to talk to him and touch his arms.

At the Panamanian plantation we walked and walked through the banana aisles in the heat. I remembered how once in Jamaica a manager had told me that banana growing had a strange, very special fascination, but I was feeling too tired to discern it. Afterwards at a buffet lunch with only water to drink a black school-teacher reminded the General of how at fourteen, after someone had stolen his bicycle, he went and saw Omar, who was then only a young major in the National Guard, and Omar had told him that there were a lot of unclaimed bicycles in the police station and he gave him a note to the police so that he was allowed to choose the best bicycle. The school-teacher finished his story, 'Now I have a chance to say thank you.' Was the young Major Torrijos already a populist or simply a kind man who liked children?

We went back to David by helicopter – all of us silent and tired, even Omar. He went to the private apartment he had there in a high-rise block and Chuchu and I to a hotel. We decided we had had enough of programming. Next day we would get off by car on our own.

It was an opportunity to revisit the Haunted House on our way back to Panama City, and even though the day was not Sunday the old man turned up while we were drinking in the bar. He was very bent with one drooping eye which looked only at the ground. He said that he couldn't let us look inside the Haunted House because he hadn't got the keys. Anyway, there was nothing to see there. A ghost? People always invented such stories about an empty house.

I ought to have asked him, 'Why has it remained empty for forty years?' but I still hoped he would let us in.

'All the same we want to take a look inside,' I said. 'When can we?'

'When will you be passing here next?'

'We can come any time you say. What about Sunday?'

'Well . . .'

'What time on Sunday?'

'Three o'clock.'

'OK.'

'But I guarantee nothing.'

We felt sure that he had no intention of being there on Sunday so we planned to turn up unexpectedly at five the next day.

In the city Chuchu and I went to the Señorial where we got excellent rum punches from Flor whose honesty and intelligence still scared Chuchu.

Chuchu's sex life was not going well. His girl friend – but which one I couldn't make out even at the time – was pregnant with only about three weeks to go. 'Now she begins to hate me,' he said. I suggested it was perhaps a bit too late in the pregnancy for love-making, but that was an idea he would not accept. 'No, no,' he said. 'She's very clever and she manages very well.' I had so far only met two of his children. I believed there were at least two others by an earlier marriage – and, of course, there was the child by the poet who owned the refrigerator and this new arrival. But I was never to know the exact origins of Chuchu's family or the number of his children, nor was he himself quite sure. To a friend who questioned him he said, 'About twelve, I think.'

Before dinner we picked up a Chilean couple whom Chuchu described as ultra-left. The man had the kind of drooping, well-meaning moustache which seems often a mark of the left wing just as a short military-style moustache belongs to the right. Chuchu had rescued the man on an occasion when he had been falsely framed for assault, or so he claimed, by the G-2 (the security police) along with a Christian Democrat leader. He went into hiding and Chuchu had taken his case to the General. The General gave a judgement worthy of Solomon. The man could either leave the country for Costa Rica, in the General's own car for safety, or he could surrender to the police in the company of Chuchu to ensure that he would suffer no ill-treatment. He decided to surrender and was condemned to a month's imprisonment, not in gaol but in the comfortable refugee apartment run by Chuchu, the Pigeon House. His wife insisted to me over dinner at the Marisco that they were not really Ultras. They had escaped from Chile at the time of Pinochet's coup.

By a curious coincidence the head of the G-2 was dining at the Marisco that night in a private room and Chuchu wanted to introduce me to him, but the idea frightened the couple. 'Another time,' the man with the weak moustache implored. 'Not when you are with us.'

That evening Chuchu described a daylight mugging which he had witnessed in the city. Two tourists were being beaten up in a street of the old town as he drove by. He stopped his car and intended to fire a shot in the air, but the men fled when they saw his revolver. 'Why didn't you fire at their legs?' I asked.

'Why should I have hurt them? They were only after money. They were poor.'

This was Panama.

To Punta Chane next day – an extraordinary non-functioning project backed by the Bank of Boston. An elaborate road system had been laid down with electric light standards and roundabouts, posters showed the future situation of hotels and banks, and yet not even a foundation stone had been laid – the road and the roundabouts led only to one or two shacks by the sea and there was no sign of work in progress. Then we drove into the hills to El Valle where in my *South American Handbook* I had read that there were trees with square trunks and golden frogs, a beautiful ride ending in disappointment – no square trees to be found and no golden frogs.

I had seen little of Omar so far on this visit. I had the impression that deliberately he was leaving me alone to see what I wanted to see, to get to know Panama in my own way, uninfluenced by him, to make my own contacts with the Sandinistas and the other refugees who had come to Panama for safety.

After my return from El Valle I had my first encounter with the Sandinistas. A young Nicaraguan doctor, Camilo, whose brother had been killed by Somoza, invited Chuchu and me to dinner. His brother had been the guerilla leader, Commandant Cero, a title which passed to his successor. Chuchu had told me before we went to the house that Somoza had sworn that he would drink Cero's blood, and Camilo was now living with his brother's Panamanian girlfriend, María Isabel. I promised not to show any knowledge of their relationship. He said I would see a photograph of the dead brother on the wall.

The photo was there all right, but there was no secrecy about their relationship. The girl was beautiful and intelligent, yet for some reason there was antagonism between her and Chuchu. Perhaps Chuchu was a little jealous of her closeness to the young Sandinista. Moreover, Chuchu had been born in Nicaragua, and the girl's grandfather had been a president of Panama, and perhaps his Mayan blood was suspicious of pure Spanish blood. He had no reason to distrust her loyalty to the Sandinista cause, but he may well have had cause to distrust her prudence. At dinner with us there was another young Sandinista, Rogelia, a mathematician like Chuchu. He was married to an Italian girl, Lidia, and Chuchu's friendship with them was to complicate still further his sexual life, for he was to marry Lidia's sister Silvana and start yet another family.

These young Sandinistas were not refugees from the guerilla war – they were part of the guerrilla war. Already a Sandinista foreign service was in existence. The young doctor would suddenly dress up in a new suit and tie and be off to Mexico on mysterious errands. When once I ran into him at the Panama airport and teased him about his smartness he told me with great seriousness, 'If you look well dressed they don't look closely at your passport.'

After his meeting with Camilo and his girl I had the impression of being taken over by the Sandinistas. Even Chuchu sank into the background. Indeed, for a day or two he disappeared entirely from the scene and I find from my diary that I began to feel resentment at always seeing the same faces – Camilo and María Isabel, the mathematician and his wife, Lidia, even the Ultras turned up again and again. Where Chuchu was I had no idea. For all I knew he was in Nicaragua or on the Costa Rican border, unloading arms from his small private plane. It was as though I were being nudged towards a frontier which I had no wish to cross on behalf of a cause which I was too ignorant to espouse. Even Omar had warned me against crossing that frontier. It would be too easy for Somoza to blame the Sandinistas for my death.

Yet I had reason to be grateful to them, for it was with María Isabel that I actually found the golden frogs in El Valle and even a square tree, after a long scramble in the forest where I was badly bitten, but more important to me she got me into the Haunted House. It was a Sunday and we had intended to fly to the San Blas Islands, but instead we drove to the bar beside the Haunted House and found it open. Within a few minutes the old man drove up.

'Let me speak to him,' María Isabel said. He had the keys in his hand, so he couldn't deny having them. His alibi was gone and María Isabel was a beautiful woman. She told him that I was an English medium who had stopped off in Panama while returning from a spiritualist conference in Australia. Rumours about his house had come to my ears.

'A lot of nonsense.'

'All the same . . .'

Grudgingly he consented to show us 'part of the house'.

He threw back a steel shutter and unlocked the heavy steel door, and we were in the living-room of the house in almost total darkness. There was no lamp and we could only see what was there with the aid of a cigarette lighter. There might be no ghost, but the house was certainly haunted by memories. Glass cases stood against the walls filled with china. Victorian pictures of women in transparent muslin robes, like reproductions of Leighton, hung between the cases. I looked through an open door into a little room which contained one steel bed, the sheets jumbled about as if the occupant had only just risen from sleep, and a bat flew out.

The old man pointed to the floor of the living-room and asked me, 'Do you know what's there?'

I hadn't the social courage to answer, 'The skeleton of a woman.'

The old man became more affable when we were again safely outside. He said there were many ghosts around, for we were standing on the gold route to Portobelo. The Spaniards had buried much gold here, and buried with the gold were the Indians who had carried it. Their spirits fought against anyone who tried to dig it up.

On parting I gave him what I thought might be taken for a Masonic sign with my fingers and he responded by calling me his brother. 'I too am a medium,' he said. 'I am a conscious one, you are *inconciente*.' I thought at first he was accusing me of being a medium without a conscience; but María Isabel explained. He meant that he could remember what had happened when he came out of a trance, while I could not.

Suddenly he realized that he had left the steel door ajar, and he scuttled back to close and double-lock it.

In the absence of Chuchu it was the Sandinistas who arranged for me to visit Hollywood, the slum lying on the edge of the American Zone. A visit, they told me, was unsafe without the escort of an inhabitant, but one of their number knew of one who would ensure our safety.

Hollywood proved to be a horrifying huddle of wooden houses sunk in rain water like scuttled boats and of communal lavatories which stank to heaven and leaked into the water around. At a sheltered corner an old woman sat selling marijuana, and we were followed step by wet step by a smoker who was half-senseless with the drug and who asked us questions which we didn't answer and wanted to lead us where our guide and protector had no wish to go.

I thought with wonder of the neat lawns, and the golf courses, and the fifty-three churches half a mile away beyond the unmarked frontier. Omar had thought of razing Hollywood to the ground and building flats (indeed, there was at least one high-rise block of flats with unlit corridors and walls streaming with moisture through which we walked with a quicker, more nervous step, seeing no one about at all), but he gave the idea up. The inhabitants of Hollywood were attached to their leaking houses which were their own, where their parents and grandparents had been born, so now he talked of 'improvements' if one day the Treaty were signed – with sanitation, running water, electric light. I couldn't believe in the possibility – touch one wall of a house, try to mend a roof and the building would surely collapse into the water at the door.

I think it may have been Hollywood which gave me a guilt-ridden night during which I dreamt that I had quarrelled with the woman I loved, and afterwards I found myself travelling by underground to the old offices of *The Times* in Queen Victoria Street in order to resign from the staff, but what right had I to resign, for hadn't I been absent for months, if not for years, on full pay?

3

Next day I returned to Colón with the young Sandinista doctor, who wanted to visit the hospital there. He too had been troubled that night by an unhappy dream – a dream of his brother who had been killed by Somoza's men. In the dream his brother had disapproved of what Camilo was doing now. I suppose he too was suffering from a sense of guilt no more rational than mine, because he was in safety while the civil war was being savagely fought in Nicaragua, but he was working under orders for his cause.

He told me a little about his brother, who had been younger than himself. His brother had been training as an engineer with Siemens in Managua, and when he was seventeen he went off on a scholarship flight to Germany. His parents never saw him again until years later the Nicaraguan police brought them from their home to identify the dead body of Commandant Cero. They had no idea that their son was the famous Cero who had struck the first serious blow against Somoza's tyranny by kidnapping in one *coup* a number of ambassadors and government ministers as they left a party and thus obtained the release of fourteen political prisoners who were all flown safely to Cuba.

My new friend Camilo knew nothing for years of what was happening to his brother after he had seen him leave for Germany as a boy. Then quite accidentally he encountered him in Mexico City and his brother had recruited him into the propaganda side of the Sandinista movement. He heard of his death on the radio in Panama.

I was glad to find when we returned to the city that Chuchu was safely back, though from where I never learnt. 'The trouble about Chuchu,' Camilo said to me, 'is that he mixes up politics with sex.' True or not, he now seemed to have a new girl friend, the wife of a gangster who was lying in hospital after a shooting affray, a rather dangerous relationship one would have thought, and in a confusing party with our Sandinista friends a pregnant girl – was it Chuchu's girl? – made her appearance, but she didn't seem to be connected with anyone there. Jokes were made about who was the father of the child.

He was killed in Vietnam, she said.

'Then you've been two years pregnant.'

'I meant in Korea.'

'That's even longer.'

She pointed at the young mathematician Rogelio.

'Well,' he said, laughing, 'who knows? It might be.'

I urged Chuchu that evening to stay sober. 'Of course I'll be sober,' he said, and he added, 'I never mix up politics with alcohol or sex.'

4

The San Blas Islands – three hundred and sixty-five of them – lie in the Atlantic off the Darién coast. The only inhabitants are Cuna Indians who live a virtually independent life. They pay no taxes. They send representatives to the National Assembly and have even negotiated their own trade treaty with Colombia. Tourists are allowed to spend a night on two of the islands. On the other three hundred and sixty-three strangers can only pass the hours of day. The San Blas lobsters are regarded very highly in Panama, yet, fresh as it was from the sea, I found mine tough and tasteless.

Far more interesting than the lobsters were the women. What interest and greed they would have aroused in the *conquistadores*, for in every nose and ear hung a gold ring. No one could tell me from whence the gold had come, for there are no gold mines in Panama. Even in the Spanish days, when the gold caravans took the trail from Panama City to Portobelo, the gold had first to be brought down the Pacific coast from Peru.

The women, quite apart from the wealth of their rings and their fashion of dressing in a rather similar style to Ancient Egyptians, were interesting to watch. The long-haired girls were unmarried: those with hair cut short were married. A distinction was made between them, even in the use of musical instruments. When they danced for us, at a fixed and very moderate fee, the unmarried rattled gourds and the married played on little bundles of pipes. They contribute to the Cuna economy by embroidering squares of material called *molas* for use as blouse fronts. That day I was with Camilo and Lidia, the wife of Rogelio. It was her birthday and she chose a *mola* for me to give her, but this was to be stolen from her a few days later under odd circumstances typical of life in Panama City.

In the evening Chuchu came to see me. He told me that Omar wanted me to go with the Panamanian delegation to Washington in five days' time for the signing of the Canal Treaty, the terms of which had at last after all these years been agreed. The *Miami Herald* that morning claimed that it was no different from the draft treaty of 1967, proposed before the General took power, but this was completely false – perhaps it was an attempt by the Americans to stir up internal trouble against Torrijos. The new Treaty would transfer immediately fifty times more territory to Panama than the old draft had done. The American military bases, it was true, were to remain until the year 2000 and only then would the Canal become entirely the property of Panama. However, the Zone, apart from these bases, would immediately cease to exist.

I felt unwilling to go to Washington. I had booked my return flight, and it was time I returned to France and to my proper work. I told Chuchu that I had no visa for the States, a white lie for it was no longer true. 'That doesn't matter,' he said, 'you will have a diplomatic passport, a Panamanian one.'

'I don't want to come back all the way here to catch my plane to Amsterdam.'

'You won't have to. The General will book you on the Concorde direct from Washington to Paris.' He said the General was already being attacked because the Treaty was not as good as people had hoped. He had made a speech to the students, saying, 'I am making what progress I can, but if I don't have the support of progressives, what can I do more?'

I gave in. 'If the General really wants me to go,' I said.

'He really wants it.'

That evening I went to the temporary home of a Nicaraguan woman writer who had been tortured by Somoza's Guardia. Only the day before she had successfully had a baby. She would say little for fear of the repercussions on her family, and one could tell from her tormented face how much she wanted to forget the past. But there were others in the room who had also suffered and were ready to talk. An Argentinian woman described the electric torture which she had endured. Another Argentinian told of a bayonet thrust up her vagina. A Peruvian

91

told of his expulsion, a Nicaraguan of his escape from a police ambush. For how many people, from how many countries in Latin America – Argentina, Chile, Nicaragua, El Salvador – Panama had become a haven of escape, thanks to the General. It had not been like this in the days of the Arias family.

5

I was suffering the result of my search in the woods of El Valle for a square tree. An irritation in my ankles kept me awake every night, so on Chuchu's advice I went to see a young black doctor at the barracks of the National Guard. He gave me a wash, a cream and some tablets and told me I had been bitten by a tiny insect called a *chitra* only too familiar to the Wild Pigs. Afterwards we went to the airport to meet a Mexican film producer who was trying to arrange the co-production of an anti-military film. He had been offered support in Mexico, Colombia, France and Cuba, but Panama was the only country which was prepared to lend him troops.

I think Chuchu's exuberance puzzled him. He had not been accustomed to deal with a security guard who was also a poet and a professor. He looked bewildered and innocent.

Camilo too was at the airport. He was smartly dressed and looked very much the young doctor, and he was off on a mysterious Sandinista errand to Mexico City. He had entrusted me some days before with a letter to an address in Paris which he wanted me to post on my return to France, but now that he knew I was going by way of Washington he was very worried about its security. 'You mustn't leave it in your luggage,' he told me. 'They are sure to search your luggage in Washington. Promise me that you'll always keep it on you, even at night.' I promised.

A man came to fetch the Mexican film producer, who had been listening with growing bewilderment to my conversation with Camilo. The 'someone' was accompanied by a quite hideous woman, a Venezuelan with dyed red hair, who seemed to me obviously in pursuit of Chuchu.

We escaped on that occasion, but nobody in Panama City only turns up once. Like a play with a small cast the same actors were always reappearing in different roles. In the course of that muddled evening I had been supposed to meet a Peruvian refugee, but the meeting was cancelled at the last moment, so I suggested to Chuchu that we should take Camilo's wife to dinner as she might be feeling lonely without him. But for some reason Chuchu couldn't find Camilo's house, though we had been there several times together, and for a yet more impenetrable reason he was convinced that María Isabel would be telephoning us at the house of Panama's ambassador to Venezuela – or was it the other way round, Venezuela's ambassador to Panama? – and the ambassador, he was sure, would give us a typical Venezuelan dinner, whatever that might signify. Of course, María Isabel didn't telephone us, it was the hideous Venezuelan woman who turned up (had Chuchu foreseen that?) and the ambassador never asked us to dinner. Indeed, I don't think he could understand what we were doing at his house. So we left, passing on the doorstep the Mexican film producer, who appeared more bewildered than ever at seeing us, and Chuchu and I had some chicken soup together at my hotel.

These last days in Panama unwound more and more quickly and confusingly. I hadn't seen Omar for some days – it was as though in the past he had been directing events and now the disorder, which involved a Mexican film producer and a Venezuelan woman and Chuchu's lapse of memory, arose from his absence. I had to get up very early the next morning because Omar wanted me to fly to a collective buffalo farm (an odd thing to find in Panama) in the mountain village of Coclesito. The farm had been started by Omar, who had built himself a small house nearby, after he had had made a forced landing in Coclesito in a helicopter and seen the hopeless isolation and poverty of the inhabitants. Their smallholdings had been washed out by a flood in which the chief's son had been drowned. What gave the General the idea of a buffalo farm I never learnt. I was fetched by María Isabel, who complained bitterly that Chuchu had made a muddle the night before over my rendezvous with the Peruvian refugee. And why on earth had we gone to the Venezuelan ambassador's house? Was it possible, I wondered, that it was because Chuchu wanted to see the hideous woman again?

Chuchu was waiting at the airport for the military plane which he had ordered and with him were a number of students from Guatemala, Ecuador and Costa Rica accompanied by their professors. Our journey to see the buffaloes was obviously meant to be an educational one, but we waited and waited and no plane arrived. Apparently the pilot, an air force officer, resented having been given orders by a mere sergeant. After two hours we sent a message to the General's secretary that it was too late now for the buffaloes and we all trooped off to the Ministry of Culture where we were joined by the two Ultras and the Sandinista mathematician, Rogelio, and we had to sit through a long and boring videotape film of Panama folk dancing. I have always detested folk dancing since I was a boy when I had watched men morris-dancing in braces. (The dances appealed particularly for some mysterious reason to their wives, who wore shot-silk dresses bought at Liberty's.)

In the middle of the film Chuchu was called away on an urgent errand. A Guatemalan professor recommended by the Dean of Guatemala University (the one who had been so drunk with Chuchu at David) had apparently been imprisoned some days before by the G-2 and charged with trying to pass forged dollar bills at the Continental Hotel.

María Isabel, the Ultras and I were invited after the film to lunch by Señor Ingram, the Minister of Culture, and while we were drinking our cocktails Chuchu arrived with the Rector of Panama University and the Guatemalan professor straight from the prison, a tall, red-haired, good-looking man of Yankee and

German origin who naturally seemed a little confused about what was happening to him. He had not expected this sudden transfer from his prison cell to drink cocktails and eat a good lunch at Panama's best restaurant. Nor could he understand what an English writer was doing there, for appparently he had read some of my books and distrusted me. He told us that he had been threatened with violence by the G-2 officers, and he had shared his cell with seven other men, including two rapists – one had killed the girl whom he had raped – and one patricide. All of them, however, had proved very sympathetic and with their professional knowledge they had helped him to smuggle a message out of prison – a message which contained the recommendation from the Dean of Guatemala University. The General, when he received it, decided that the whole affair was probably a plot by the Guatemalan police against a professor who was known to be left-wing, so he at once ordered his release, but a discreet one by means of Chuchu, and he thought it wiser all the same for the professor to return after a few days of relaxation to Guatemala. What we saw of the professor later made me doubt whether he was quite as innocent as he had claimed.

This continued to prove one of my more confusing Panamanian days. Nothing went quite right, and I soon began to feel just as bewildered as the Guatemalan professor and the Mexican film producer. Chuchu and I had planned to dine together on something more substantial this time than chicken soup. He asked me, 'Do you mind if I bring the thin girl [the gangster's wife] to dinner? I want to sleep with her tonight.' He telephoned and I heard him say that we would be outside the block where she lived in five minutes.

Round and round the block we drove and no one came, so we went to a café, where a group of reactionaries were drinking and maligning the General. I joined them and argued the other way while Chuchu went and telephoned again. He came back crestfallen. A strange woman's voice had told him that the girl was asleep, but he couldn't help wondering with whom.

So we dined instead with Rogelio and Lidia, and of course the Guatemalan professor turned up a second time – the Sandinistas had agreed to give him lodging because he didn't want to be alone, since he was still scared of the G-2. He planned to return to Guatemala in two days' time and he had arranged for a lot of people to be at the airport to meet him in case he disappeared with no one knowing. Would the Dean of the University, I asked, be there? He thought he would.

In the lift going to my bedroom I was greeted by a National Guard officer in a very friendly way. I checked later with Chuchu who was suspicious of some of the National Guard officers.

'He told me he was Colonel Diaz,' I said.

Chuchu reassured me. 'The best man after the General.'

I was not to meet him again for five years and then he would be head of security and the General dead.

6

Next day the plane really took off for Coclesito with the professors and students. The landing strip was only just long enough for us to touch down. It was extremely hot, the village was ankle-deep in mud, the buffaloes were as uninteresting as buffaloes always are and the deep forest lay all around. The girl students and the professors bathed in the river and some of the buffaloes bathed too. The river looked almost ready to flood again. The collective farm provided quite a tasty lunch, but there was nothing except water to quench the thirst.

I looked into the village church. It was falling into ruin and there was a chicken run in the aisle. I remembered what the General had said about neglected cemeteries – here certainly was a neglected church, and I thought unkindly of Archbishop McGrath of Panama. Had he so many churches to look after in the Republic that he couldn't pay a visit to a village where the General had bothered to build himself a small house? No priest had visited the place for the last year. The people looked to the General and not to the Church for a measure of help. I asked how many days of rain there were in the average year. 'You don't ask how many days of rain,' I was told, 'you ask how many days without rain and the answer is four.'

Dinner that night back in Panama City was at the flat of a Brazilian refugee, and my suspicion about Chuchu was partly confirmed, for he arrived with the awful Venezuelan woman – was he again in the toils of his tenderness? Among the guests was also an exiled Peruvian general who had been President of the Socialist Party. He told me that in Peru he had had a hundred tanks under his command and he could easily have carried out a *coup*, but he gave up and went into exile for the sake of 'military honour'. I was glad to think that 'military honour' had not stood in the way of Omar Torrijos in 1968, or probably few of these refugees would have been alive.

Time was running out, and I felt the same emotion as the year before, a mixture of impatience for home and regret at leaving. Omar had booked me, as he had promised, from Washington to Paris on the Concorde and he was arranging my Panamanian diplomatic passport. Now he was shut away in the house of Rory González, writing his speech for the signing of the Treaty, and for the time being he was unapproachable.

I had seen less of him than the year before, but my affection had grown. I was beginning to appreciate what he had done and what he had risked in trying to achieve his dream for a Central America which would be socialist and not Marxist, independent of the United States and yet not a menace to her. I felt for him as for a teacher as well as a friend. I was learning from him, even when he was absent, some of the problems of Central America.

The day before we left for Washington Chuchu and I went to the airport to meet Gabriel García Márquez, the Colombian novelist, who was to be another foreign member of the Panamanian delegation. It was a day of drenching rain and his plane was indefinitely delayed. We left a message that he would find us at the Peruvian restaurant, the Pez de Oro, and we just had time for two pisco sours, a drink I had learnt to enjoy in Chile, Allende's Chile, before the telephone rang. The General was asking for me urgently.

I found him in a small room in González's house, bent over a manuscript – his speech for Washington. There was no question here of a ghosted speech. His handwriting was becoming almost as illegible as mine with his corrections.

'I am nervous,' he said, 'but Carter is more nervous and that comforts me a little.' He told me the story of a Bolivian officer – why Bolivian? – going into action. He found his feet were trembling, so he addressed them, 'You sons of a bitch, this is nothing to what you are going to feel later.'

He was unhappy that Carter had invited the South American military dictators to the ceremony of signing – Videla of Argentina, Pinochet of Chile, Banzer of Bolivia, Stroessner of Paraguay, the President of Guatemala. He would have preferred only those moderate leaders who had supported him in his long negotiations, from Colombia, Venezuela and Peru. But Carter had insisted on inviting the whole bunch – except for Fidel Castro, whom Omar would gladly have welcomed, if only for his wise and aggravating counsel of prudence which had led at last to the Treaty. Somoza in Nicaragua had refused, being fully occupied with civil war, and Haiti was to be represented only by her ambassador.

Omar read me his speech. He was a little nervous of the wicked and amusing way in which he planned to begin it. I encouraged him, but I was not certain that he would stick to his admirable text when he reached Washington. I even added one sentence of my own, but, alas, I can no longer remember that little entry of mine into history. I was also able to show him the right spot to introduce a good idea of his for which he had been unable to find a place and which he was ready to abandon.

I have a vivid memory of him crouched over his unfamiliar work, worried and unsure of himself. These are the most enduring memories I have of Omar: the young beginner at the art of writing who was finding the choice of words difficult; the visitor to his home town rocking back and forth on the porch of the garage mechanic in Santiago who had been his schoolboy friend; and one other memory which was to be planted three years later of a man tired out, perhaps a little drunk, fallen asleep with his head on the shoulder of his young mistress, who had recently borne him a child.

That evening was the last of my stay in Panama, and Chuchu and I had dinner with Rogelio and Lidia. The Guatemalan professor had left for his own country, and he had taken with him the piece of embroidery which I had given to Lidia on the San Blas island, returning their hospitality with a petty theft.

7

Next day, as we flew over Cuba, Omar sent his greetings by radio to Fidel Castro, although Carter had refused to invite Castro to Washington. Omar was a man who was faithful to his friends, even when he did not fully share their politics.

We landed in the dark at the military aerodrome outside Washington at eight o'clock. A Marine guard of honour, the glare of television lights, Secretary of State Vance waiting to greet Omar at the end of a long narrow strip of red carpet, the two national anthems which seemed to go on for ever as we of the delegation stood cramped together on the carpet – I had never pictured myself arriving in this fashion in the States, where for a long time I had been refused more than a three weeks' visa.

A ninety-dollar suite waited for me at the Sheraton with an enormous sitting-room and a poster by Chagall of Vence, a town close to my home in Antibes, hanging over the desk. At the sight of the picture I felt lonely and sick for France. Omar and Chuchu were far away at the Panamanian Embassy, and I wondered whether I would ever see them again except at a great distance in the hall where the Treaty would be signed. I went downstairs to hurry up the slow arrival of my luggage, and it was strange to me to hear nothing but American spoken around me, when I was so used now to Spanish voices. That night I went unhappily to bed, having put Camilo's letter in my pyjama pocket. I tried the radio – there was an interview on abortion. I tried another channel – it was a talk about the conversion of sewage. Sleep was better.

Things improved next day. With García Márquez I went to lunch at the Panamanian Embassy and found myself again among familiar faces. Omar was very cheerful after a meeting with Carter. Carter had asked him how to deal with all the dictators who had converged on Washington and he had replied, 'Just refuse them any arms.'

Was it at this meeting that Omar broke down and wept in his wife's arms – Carter has described the scene in his memoirs – or was it the next day, immediately before the ceremony of signing the Treaty at which Omar seemed quite composed? I was not surprised when I read of his tears at the moment when the dream which he had been pursuing for so long seemed on the point of coming true. One had always been conscious in him of a sensibility which he held sternly in check, a sensibility which had to find relief from time to time in the company of a friend whom he trusted (he trusted Carter) or after enough glasses of Black Label. Then it would flash out in a moment of unrestrained self-exposure, just as when I had asked him what was his most recurring dream and he had replied, without hesitating for a second, 'Death.' Chuchu told me some years later that he had often seen Omar weep, and perhaps one of the reasons I grew to love him was the complete absence in him of Latin *macho*.

Omar told me that he had got on well with Jordan, the President's aide, and Vice-President Mondale too, who owned a baseball bat which had been signed for him in the States by a famous Panamanian player. Mondale said jokingly to the General that he had intended to give it him as a present, but then he thought it would be inadvisable to bring it with him to the White House in case he was accused of threatening to use a big stick.

These were the honeymoon hours of the Treaty which was to be signed next day. The Treaty had been passed by Congress and the General had not fully foreseen the way in which it was to be tampered with by the Senate after the signing. The two signatures on the paper had seemed to him, as to all Panamanians, to be virtually the end of the affair. When serious revisions were made later by the Senate it was like a betrayal. Indeed, even in Europe we find it difficult to understand how the heads of state can hold a solemn meeting to sign a treaty which has been passed by Congress and then see it altered after the signature by the Senate – all this parade of dictators and delegations meaning nothing final.

There were to be two demonstrations in the streets of Washington that night, one against the Treaty and one against the presence of Pinochet in Washington. García Márquez asked me to go with him to the demonstration against Pinochet and unwillingly I refused. I didn't trust the American people to distinguish between one Latin American general and another.

During the evening in the hall of the Organization of American States there was a gigantic reception for the heads of state and their delegations, with loaded buffets sufficient for one thousand guests. There was hardly standing room on the first two floors around the buffets, so the charming young Panamanian woman who was looking after me led me to the second floor where there was no food and therefore enough space to turn round in. There too I was more likely to encounter at least one of the dictators. The dictators would hardly be fighting for food around the buffets. I decided if I had the good fortune to encounter Pinochet I would say to him, 'We have, I believe, an acquaintance in common . . . Doctor Allende.'

However, Pinochet was not to be seen, but Videla was there and the Guatemalan President, both in civilian clothes looking democratic, and I took up my stand a few feet away from Stroessner of Paraguay who was also wearing a suit. I had seen

101

him last in 1968 on the National Day in Asunción when he was dressed in a general's uniform and stood on a platform to salute the crippled survivors of the unnecessary Bolivian war as they trundled by in wheeled chairs and the colonels stood stiffly upright in their cars like ninepins in a bowling alley. Now, out of his uniform, he looked more than ever like the flushed owner of a German *bierstube*. He was surrounded by a subservient group who seemed to be hanging on his words, but perhaps they were playing a part and they were really bodyguards, there for his protection. I thought: If I had a gun and were suicidal how easy it would be to rid the world of one tyrant.

A man was passing by us to join Stroessner's group when he was stopped by my companion. She began to say, 'This is one of General Stroessner's ministers. May I introduce . . .' – we each of us put out a polite hand – 'This is Mr Graham Greene.' The minister's hand dropped and left mine to reach after it through the empty air. 'You passed once through Paraguay,' he accused me in a tone of fury and went on to join his general. I couldn't help feeling a little proud that apparently I had been able to arouse the dislike of one more dictator. I had experienced much the same pride when Doctor Duvalier published a pamphlet in Haiti with the bilingual title, *'Graham Greene démasqué: Graham Greene Finally Exposed'*.

Except for Stroessner's minister everyone I spoke to in that huge gathering from the Latin American states was unexpectedly friendly. A writer who travels far from home does not expect friendliness. His work probably offends more people than it pleases. For a foreigner to write with inadequate experience of their countries is justifiably resented by those who are native born. I was happy that evening to meet Mexicans who praised *The Power and the Glory* and Argentinians who praised *The Honorary Consul*.

Next morning I had a call from Archbishop McGrath of Panama and we agreed to go together to the signing of the Treaty. In the car he told me of a prayer which he had written specially for the occasion in case he was called on to open the proceedings. He even recited it to me and I couldn't help thinking of the chickens in the aisle of the ruined church he had never bothered to visit, but in fact no such prayer was invited. He struck me then as one of those agreeable ecclesiastics whose tone of voice never varies and who knows in advance exactly how much and how little he wants to impart. The church at Coclesito belonged to the same country but not to the same world as the Archbishop. The Archbishop was accompanied by a layman who looked like his name – Quigley. I can make use of that name, I thought, one day, in God knows what story.

8

It was certainly a Great Spectacular, the signing of the Canal Treaty. We sat in blocks of countries and Panama adjoined the Senatorial block of the United States, with Venezuela on our other flank. We, the Panamanians, were a mixed bag, including not only myself and García Márquez, but more suitably the mother of a student killed by the Marines in the great riot of '64.

I had seen nothing like it as a star vehicle since *Round the World in Eighty Days*. All the familiar actors from how many television screens and newspaper photographs seemed to be there – all except Elizabeth Taylor. Kissinger, before the delegation had settled into their seats, could be seen buttonholing his way around the hall of the Organization of American States with his world-wide grin; five rows in front of me I could see Nelson Rockefeller being strenuously amiable to Ladybird, as though the two of them were sitting out a dance together, and ex-President Ford was in the same row, more blond than I had imagined him from the screen – or had he been to the barber? There too were Mr and Mrs Mondale, Mrs Carter . . . Two rows in front of me sat Andy Young, bright and boyish. All of them were looking consciously unimportant like the stars in *Round the World*, who had accepted minor parts for the joke of it all.

They were not there really to act, only to be noticed, like partygoers having a night out together, pleased to feel at home with friendly faces – 'What, *you* here?'

The important character actors were up on the platform – an unpleasant sight but more impressive than the stars below: General Stroessner of Paraguay, General Videla of Argentina with a face squashed into such a narrow space that there was hardly room for his two foxy eyes, General Banzer of Bolivia, a little frightened man with an agitated moustache – he had been miscast and misdressed.

There too was the greatest character actor of them all – General Pinochet himself – the man you love to hate. Like Boris Karloff, he really had attained the status of instant recognition; he was the one who could look down with amused contempt at the highly paid frivolous Hollywood types below him. His chin was so deeply sunk in his collar that he seemed to have no neck at all; he had clever, humorous, falsely good-fellow eyes which seemed to be telling us not to take too seriously all those stories of murder and torture emanating from South America. I could hardly believe that only a week had passed since I listened in Panama to the refugee who broke down when she described how a bayonet had been thrust into her vagina. Hovering behind the dictators was old Bunker, the Refrigerator, keeping an anxious eye on *his* Treaty, sucking dry lips. He looked like an old, old stork who had been given human features in a children's book – his head stuck out a long way in advance of his body.

Pinochet, I feel sure, knew how he dominated the scene – he was the only one against whom people were protesting in the streets of Washington with banners – perhaps they couldn't spell Stroessner's name and they couldn't even remember Banzer's. Pinochet was tactful, he didn't wave to his ally Kissinger down below, and Kissinger never looked up at him. Then we all stood for the two national anthems as Carter and General Torrijos entered to sign the Treaty, a treaty a bit shop-soiled as it had been fingered and corrected for thirteen years, yet I feel sure I was not the only one who continued to watch Pinochet. Like Karloff he didn't need to have a speaking part – he didn't even need to grunt.

Carter looked miserably unhappy. He made a banal little speech and was almost inaudible from five rows back in spite of all the microphones. But as a temporary Panamanian I felt proud of Omar Torrijos, who spoke in a voice very unlike Carter's with an edge which cut the silence. To my relief he began the text as he had read it to me, abruptly, with no conventional 'Mr President, Your Excellencies, etc.' so that even the stars below the platform began to listen. It sounded for a moment as though he were attacking the very Treaty that he was about to sign.

'The Treaty is very satisfactory, vastly advantageous to the United States, and we must confess not so advantageous to Panama.'

A pause and the General added, 'Secretary of State Hay, 1903.'

It was a good joke to play on the Senators who were there in force and were not amused, but it was a good deal more than a joke. Torrijos was signing the new Treaty with reluctance; as he had once said to me, it was only 'to save the lives of forty thousand young Panamanians'. Two clauses of the Treaty particularly stuck in his gullet; the delay till the year 2000 for complete Panamanian control of the Canal and the clause which would allow the United States to intervene even after that date if the Canal's neutrality were endangered. He would not, I thought, be entirely unhappy if the Senate refused to ratify the Treaty; he would be left then with the simple solution of violence which had often been in his mind, with desire and apprehension balanced as in a sexual encounter.

The United States was lucky to be dealing with Omar Torrijos, a patriot and an idealist who had no formal ideology, except a general preference for Left over Right and a scorn for bureaucrats. His position was a difficult one, for he was a solitary man without the base of a political party, and the

105

old parties continued to exist in his shadow – the Christian Democrats consisting of the bourgeoisie who hated him, the Communists who gave him, if only for the moment, a tactical support, the extreme left groups who were all against the Treaty (ironically for much the same reason as the General). He could trust the younger officers of the National Guard, and he could depend on the Wild Pigs – that was about all. Of some senior officers of the Guard one had to speak with more caution. If the Treaty were not ratified Panama would need the General, and his position and his popularity would be secure. If the Treaty were ratified, the General's future and Panama's future would be far more dubious, and so it proved.

With ratification more than three hundred square miles of valuable real estate would be returned immediately to Panama – and a great deal of cash. Plenty of pockets were ready to be lined. Their owners were not interested in the General's plan for free school meals and free milk for all children, for the elimination of the slums in Colón and Panama City, for an orphanage and a pleasure park for the poor who were now condemned to spend their leisure hours in such horrifying districts as Hollywood. The landlords of Panama City – and they included a few high-ranking army officers – were likely to have other ideas. The General's life if the Treaty were ratified would be a poor risk for an insurance company, for he was not a man who could be flown like a politician to Miami. It was little wonder that he dreamt a good deal of death and that his dreams were reflected in his eyes.

There were eight other generals of the southern hemisphere on the platform to watch Torrijos sign this treaty which he didn't like, and I think many demonstrators in Washington confused them together – they were all generals, they were all in some way dictators, a protest against Pinochet was a protest against the whole lot. Omar was well aware of that danger. He had wanted, as I have written, only the more reputable leaders to be present, but Carter had insisted on his invitation to all the members of the Organization of American States. Carter's insistence was a triumph for Pinochet and an embarrassment for Torrijos.

After the signing of the Treaty Carter and Torrijos set off down the platform in opposite directions to greet the heads of state. An embrace is the usual friendly greeting in Latin America, but I noticed how Torrijos embraced only the leaders of Colombia, Venezuela and Peru and confined himself to a formal handshake with Bolivia and Argentina as he worked down the row towards Pinochet. But Pinochet had noticed that too, and his eyes gleamed wickedly with amusement. When his turn came he grasped the hand of Torrijos and flung his arm around his shoulder. If any journalist's camera clicked at that moment it would appear that Torrijos had embraced Pinochet.

Next day before catching the Concorde to Paris I spoke with Chuchu, as I thought yet again for the last time. He was unhappy about the Treaty. It wasn't good enough and there was still the Senate . . . He spoke of resigning from the security guard and returning to the University.

'Stay for six months,' I pleaded with him. 'The greatest danger to Omar will come when the Treaty is ratified. He needs you. There's no one else he can trust.' Chuchu did stay, but all the same it was not in his power to save Omar. As he had said to me in the motel, 'A revolver is no defence.'

Flying home I said a final goodbye as I believed to this odd interlude in my life. For two years Omar had wanted a friendly observer while he fought for the Treaty. Now the Treaty had been signed and any use I might be to him was over. No more Omar, no more Chuchu, I told myself in the Concorde, and the discomfort of the Concorde matched my sad mood. The steward couldn't even produce a bit of cheese as we pelted towards Paris faster than sound – 'Only by special request.'

'This is a special request.'

They dug up a small stale triangle of Camembert.

In my pocket in safety lay Camilo's letter.

PART III
1978

1

I was far away in Antibes, reading only in newspapers of the civil war in Nicaragua. Hardly a day passed without a paragraph which reminded me of my Sandinista friends in Panama. Then suddenly one day Panama and Nicaragua came unexpectedly to Antibes in the person of the young mathematician Rogelio. He was ringing from the station at Nice and he was on his way to Italy. Apparently he needed a visa for Italy and he had none, but this didn't worry him unduly. After all, he had an Italian wife. One could always arrange things like visas, he said over the telephone, but he would like to break his journey and have a talk with me.

I found him a room for the night and we dined together. I felt hungry for news. He told me that Camilo had at last seen action with a group of Sandinistas who had crossed the Costa Rican frontier. It had not been a successful foray, for they had been attacked from the air and they had no anti-aircraft guns. Now Rogelio was on a mission to raise money for arms. He gave me the name and number of an account in Panama City in case I knew of any rich sympathizers. There was no problem, he said, about small arms. They could capture enough of these from Somoza's National Guard. It was anti-aircraft guns which were needed. Alas! I was of little use to him. I could only send off a small cheque of my own to Panama in the hope that it would buy a few bullets, one of which might put paid to Somoza.

2

A few more weeks passed and another familiar voice was speaking over the telephone late one evening in July.

'Where are you, Chuchu?'

'In Panama, of course. Where do you expect me to be? When are you arriving? The General wants to know. KLM have your ticket.'

I was very much surprised by the invitation, and I calculated with haste. '9.30 in the morning on 19 August. Will that do?'

But I very nearly missed the plane.

It was early morning on the eighteenth, and I was staying at the Ritz in London en route to Amsterdam – the hotel where in those days something always went wrong, which was one of the reasons why I liked it. Writing is for most of the time a lonely and unsatisfying occupation. One is tied to a table, a chair, a stack of paper. Only a strict discipline enabled me to carry on, so that I welcomed the unexpected which the Ritz seemed always ready to supply – smoked salmon, perhaps, served instead of eggs for breakfast, a bird flapping all day in the chimney, a window which could not be opened or else could not be closed, an Egyptian waiter, who was studying to play the drums and who tried to kiss the girl next door when he brought her breakfast. So it was in the good old days before Trafalgar House bought the hotel and hung hideous pictures in the corridors and made the service dully reliable. All the same, in the early morning of 18 August things seemed to be going just a bit too far.

I woke coughing heavily and turned on the light, but I couldn't even see to the other end of my bedroom through an evil-smelling and throat-tickling smoke. I looked out of the window and then hastily, and with the usual great difficulty, closed it. A building which was under construction next door had been left covered in plastic and the plastic was on fire. Firemen could be seen down below carrying torches and wearing gas-masks. It was their shouts which had luckily woken me. I opened the door on to the passage to let the smoke escape and saw a receptionist with a fireman coming down the corridor. He offered to change my room, but as the smoke was clearing and I was all packed for Panama, I preferred to stay where I was, coughing. The cough was to stay with me all through the next two weeks until I returned to Europe.

Later that day I caught my plane bound, so I believed, for Amsterdam – it was the first time in my life that I had got on the wrong plane – with all the checking of tickets and boarding cards a difficult thing to do. I only discovered I was on the wrong plane when a steward announced that we were landing on time in Rotterdam. I think perhaps the smoke had got a little into my brain as well as into my throat, and I began to think that the Fates had decided against Panama. My plane from Amsterdam was due to leave in a little over an hour.

I rushed through immigration and customs and took a taxi, but I had no guilders. I explained my predicament only after we drove off. The driver took it well: 'What currency have you got?'

'French,' I said, 'some English and a few American dollars.'

He chose the dollars and I thought I would lose a lot on the exchange, but no – he rang up a currency exchange office on the car radio and found the correct rate.

The Fates ceased to be against me. I just caught my plane – no time to enjoy the Van Gogh lounge – and at nine in the morning Panama time (half an hour early) I was welcomed by Chuchu at the new international airport which I was seeing for the first time. Chuchu had left his car at the national airport and brought his own small plane (thirteen years old, he told me) to fly us back to his car. I had little confidence in a poet and professor as a pilot and wondered whether the Fates had yet another card to play. Bernard Diederich, Chuchu said, was at the hotel waiting for me and the General wanted us to be at Farallón, his house by the Pacific, next morning. 'I will fly the two of you,' Chuchu said. 'There's just room for two passengers in the plane.'

'Couldn't we go by road?'

'Impossible. The General wants you there by nine.'

I don't think Diederich next morning enjoyed the flight any more than I did. Panama weather is unpredictable and the rainy season was approaching. On the flight Chuchu was in a philosophical mood. 'If shit was worth money,' he reflected suddenly out of the blue, 'the poor would be born without arses.'

Omar was in bed with a fever when we arrived, but he soon joined us. He was relaxed and talkative as he lay, as he always liked to do, in his hammock. I owe to Diederich the substance of his talk, for he recorded it.

After the signing of the Canal Treaty ex-President Arias had been allowed to return to his estates in Chiriquí near the Costa Rican border, and on his arrival two months ago in Panama City he had addressed a great gathering, who were drawn perhaps more by curiosity than by sympathy, in Santa Ana Park. He had attacked Torrijos with a venom which at least helped to prove that there was freedom of speech in Panama.

Watching Omar as he talked to me now from his hammock, I remembered the speech of Arias which I had read the previous evening on the plane. Arias had drawn a portrait of Omar as a tyrant who had flung his enemies out of aeroplanes and tortured prisoners. No names of these 'disappeared' victims had ever been published anywhere, no widows had paraded the streets of Panama City as they had in Buenos Aires, for of course the disappeared did not exist. A political dissident had only to cross from one side of the street in Panama to the other to find safety. Arias had based his picture of Torrijos's Panama on reports of Videla's Argentina and Pinochet's Chile, while he sat in his safe home in Miami. In his speech he had spoken of Omar as a 'psychopath who should be in an insane asylum', and at that moment the 'psychopath' lay there in his hammock cheerfully discussing his future with us.

'I'm going to give the politicians a big surprise. I'm designing a system – a political party – in order to get out. They think I am

114

designing a system to stay in. The politicians are aiming their guns in the wrong direction. They will waste their ammunition and then they will say, "But the son of a bitch is unpredictable."' He gave a smile of mischief. 'All I want is a house, rum and a girl.'

'As if the wickedness and infamy of the principal traitor were not enough' – it was ex-President Arias who now was speaking in my memory – 'he has sold the fatherland for a few coins just as Judas sold Our Lord Jesus Christ and, like Judas, he tries in his ignorance to flee his own conscience, putting himself to sleep with alcoholic beverages' (perhaps he should have added 'Black Label, usually at weekends') 'and narcotics' (these were presumably the good Havana cigars sent to him by Fidel). 'Do not be surprised when he is found hanging from some tree in his own back yard.'

Omar rocked himself to and fro in the hammock with one leg. He said, 'I don't even know whether I have done good or bad. It's like going to the gas station. You pay and the pump returns to zero. Every time I wake up I'm back to zero.'

Again I was listening to Arias. 'For almost ten years we have been in exile, looking from our humble patio in Florida towards the south, towards our beloved Panama, reflecting and meditating, with a single hope and a single prayer . . .'

I asked Omar what he thought of Arias. 'He's a political archaeological piece,' Omar said. 'You look at it once in the museum, but you don't trouble to look twice.'

He went on, 'There is a political emptiness here. The struggle for the Canal Treaty has left us with this feeling of emptiness. To fill it we must turn to the internal front. We must organize a political party for the elections we are going to hold. I am for social democracy. I've talked with Felipe González in Spain, with Colombia and the Dominican Republic. I caught this damn cold there at the inauguration of Guzmán. Of course, if Arias and the oligarchy return to power we are in a bit of trouble.' He laughed. 'We have broken all the laws of the constitution – *their* constitution.'

115

His new party was to be called the PRD – the Democratic Revolutionary Party. Its foundation would be announced officially on 11 October, the tenth anniversary of his military *coup*. At the same time the ban on the other political parties would be lifted, but the ban had never been a complete one. It had only meant that every candidate during elections, whether he were conservative, socialist, liberal or Communist, fought as an individual candidate without a party label.

He went on, 'I feel too old to talk about the future.' (He was still a man in his forties.) 'The future belongs to youth. A party is necessary to me now because I'm tired and bored with politics – internal politics. You see, when people find a leader they work him to death like a peasant works a good ox to death. The peasants speak to me frankly, and the peasant knows you have a limp even when you may be curled up in a hammock or lying down with a sheet over you.'

I asked him about the Treaty. I knew he was bitterly disappointed by the amendments made in the Senate and that he was criticized by his own left. He said, 'My idea of the ultra-left is this: when they face the impossibility of making *their* revolution, they make a cowardly escape by planning a future revolution which never becomes a reality. In this country we don't even have two million inhabitants. There is no reason to pay a high price for social change. If it is not necessary, why do it? I don't support a radical position in this little country.'

He referred to the American fear of Communism in Angola. He said, 'I told Andrew Young that Africa is more a danger to your vanity than to your security. There is no danger in Africa. It's a continent which still hasn't found a personality. Fifty years from now people in little Volkswagens will cruise happily down the highways and observe the beauty of the jungle and forget the tractors that the jungle swallowed up.'

He had digested his disappointment over the Treaty and had even begun to minimize its importance. He said, 'In fourteen months from now they will give us two-thirds of the land in the

116

Canal Zone, and we will receive thirty cents – a notable increase – for every ship using the Canal until we take control in the year 2000. But more important than the Canal is our copper development. Until now we've only exported bananas and sovereignty.' (By sovereignty he meant the Panama flag and the tax-evading international companies.) 'We will export copper by 1983.' (This was a prophecy that failed to come true.) 'Then there is our hydro-electric capacity. Soon we will have one kilowatt per inhabitant.'

He went back to the question of the Canal. 'The Canal began with fourteen thousand workers and it still has fourteen thousand. We have no ports and because of this it costs us seventeen dollars a ton to export our products. When we have the Canal we can export more. We have a new cement factory which is penalized because we can't export. We can't put up the Canal tolls further, so it's on the flanks of the Canal that we must develop.'

I remembered what he had told the schoolchildren the year before, that he was not going to exchange white landlords for coffee-coloured ones. I asked, 'Is there going to be a land grab?'

'No, no,' he said, 'we are going to be careful of the Zone resources. We can't change the land much. The forests are needed to provide the watershed for the Canal.'

I went back to my room in Panama City and I reread President Arias's speech. '11 October 1968, a fatal day on which Satanic treason, inspired by lasciviousness, covetousness and envy swept our beloved land, covering it with groans, pain and blood . . .'

I thought of 'the monster', of the 'Judas' in his hammock and I thought also of the fisherman who was in the habit of walking regularly up the beach at weekends past the guard and shouting drunken insults at Omar sitting on his verandah, but on the return journey, sobered by his walk, he would go by in silence. Omar was delighted by this weekend ritual, especially when it was performed in front of such serious and important guests as

117

Mr Bunker and the American delegation. I wondered how President Arias would have reacted in his days of power.

3

In the evening I went to a bad Nicaraguan meal with my Sandinista friends and I met for the first time the poet, Father Ernesto Cardenal, who is now the Minister of Culture in Nicaragua. I thought him perhaps a trifle consciously charismatic with his white beard and his flowing white hair and the blue beret on top, and he seemed a little conscious of his own romantic character as a priest, a Communist and a refugee from Somoza, who had destroyed his monastery on an island in the Great Lake. Next evening we met again at the house of Camilo and María Isabel at a birthday party for one of the Sandinista guerrilla leaders, Pomares, whose life had been saved by Omar. He had been captured in Honduras and was about to be deported to Nicaragua and certain death when the General intervened.

It seemed an oddly juvenile party for a guerrilla leader: there was a birthday cake and everyone sang 'Happy birthday to you', and the faces were nearly all as familiar to me now as family faces, and old Father Cardenal beamed from the background like a grandfather and the guerrilla extinguished two sets of candles, each in one blow, and I thought he was a little embarrassed by the cake and the candles. He gave me the impression of a genuine fighter surrounded by amateurs. A few days later he returned to Nicaragua and was killed in action. Now in Managua Somoza's former headquarters, known as the Bunker, is named after him.

Father Cardenal tried to persuade me to go over to Nicaragua, but I couldn't help feeling that my death there would prove a too-easy gift for propaganda. Either side would be able to blame the other and my death would be more valuable than any other service that I could render, and quite possibly it might

118

be rendered to the wrong side. Anyway, I knew the General was against my going. He believed that the civil war was reaching a climax. So I preferred to be a tourist and went off next day by helicopter to the legendary city of my imagination, Nombre de Dios: a small clearing, too small for a plane to land, and an Indian village of a few dozen huts. Not even a piece of ruined wall marked what had once been a greater port than Vera Cruz, one which had been named by Columbus Puerto de Bastimentos, the Harbour of Provisions, and which had been sacked by Francis Drake – he mistakenly left a lot of silver ingots behind.

When we got back to Panama we found that the General's forecast of the war in Nicaragua had been in some sort confirmed. There had been an outbreak in Managua, the capital, and the National Palace had been seized by a small group of a dozen Sandinistas, who were holding a thousand deputies and officials hostage and demanding the release of their comrades in prison.

A dream that night depressed me so much that I woke bored and unhappy. I wanted to be back in Europe, I didn't know why. However, one thing remained to be done before I went home and that was the long-delayed trip to Bocas del Toro, so uninvitingly described in the *South American Handbook*, and Chuchu agreed to come with me the next day. But it was not to be. All our plans were changed and at the same time our spirits were raised by Omar, who had tracked us down to where we were having dinner in an Italian restaurant which we had never visited before. Somehow he had discovered our whereabouts. Chuchu was wanted on the telephone.

He came back excited and, like me, a little drunk. The General was sending an army plane to Managua early next morning – probably at five – to pick up the Sandinista commando, the released prisoners and some of their hostages, and we were to go in the plane. We should be at the airport by four. Life had become interesting again.

Next morning we arrived just on time, but the plane had left

119

an hour before, for Chuchu had failed to understand, or else the telephone had failed to communicate, the General's advice that we spend the night at the airport. Chuchu found himself in disgrace. He was told firmly to hold himself 'on disposition' – which presumably meant staying at home by his telephone in a sort of house arrest. As for me I tried to kill a long day with reading and sleep, until he finally rejoined me, as depressed as myself. We had been summoned by the General to Rory's house.

We thought it best to have some rum punches first, made by Flor at the Señorial bar, for we expected a reprimand. But not a bit of it. Omar was in great good humour. He had decided to send me with Chuchu on a mission to Belize to see George Price, the Prime Minister. This was part of his determination to be my tutor in the affairs of Central America, not only in the affairs of Panama. He had become fond of Price – a strange friendship, for the two men could hardly have differed more in character, though in politics they were both moderate social-ists. The friendship began when Panama supported Belize against its enemy Guatemala at the United Nations and persuaded Venezuela to do the same – the only two Latin American countries to oppose Guatemala.

The Foreign Minister was with the General and he sketched out for us the situation in Belize, where the Conservative opposition were opposed to the independence which Price sought, since they believed that it might involve the removal of the sixteen hundred British troops serving as a trip wire against a Guatemalan invasion. Price wished to remain inside the Commonwealth, but he would have preferred to substitute Commonwealth troops for British. Guatemala might be sat-isfied with a small surrender of territory giving access to the sea, but then would Mexico on her northern frontier demand the same? In which case what would be left of Belize?

'You will like Price,' Omar told me. 'He's a man after your own heart. He wanted to be a priest, not a prime minister.'

In the morning, before the usual Panamanian muddle started over our journey, I went to see the Sandinista commando and the released prisoners, who included Tomás Borge, who is now a good friend to me, at the military base of a unit called the Tigers. The leader of the commando, Eden Pastora, had the handsome face of a film star, and he was being interviewed for American television by a particularly stupid journalist. 'Is it true that Carter wrote you a letter? When will you be going back to Nicaragua?' The lights flashed and the cameras clicked. Perhaps it was at that moment, when he became aware of an audience of millions, that Pastora's corruption began, so that four years later he turned against his fellow Sandinistas. After their victory they were to appoint him commander of the *milice*, the villagers who were being trained in self-defence, a sort of home guard, but not commander of the army; he was appointed the Vice-Minister of Defence and not the Minister, and yet his extraordinary exploit in capturing the National Palace with a handful of men had made him more famous outside Nicaragua than Daniel Ortega, the chief of the Junta, Humberto Ortega, the head of the army, or even Tomás Borge, now the Minister of the Interior.

There must inevitably have been many wounded vanities when the civil war ended, and the two vanities which did most harm to the Sandinista cause proved to be those of Pastora and Archbishop Obando. (The Archbishop had negotiated the terms of the hostages' release with Somoza and he was on the same plane to Panama as Pastora so as to guarantee the safety of the commando.)

Now, as I half-expected would happen, everything which had been arranged for our visit to Belize began to go wrong. Camilo telephoned me in the evening to tell me that Chuchu after all couldn't go with me. Some Frenchman whom I didn't know would take his place. I got angry (I suspected unjustly some Sandinista interference) and I told Camilo that I would prefer to go back to Europe. I had been long enough away. Camilo seemed to agree and said that he would pick me up next morning and take me to KLM for my ticket, but next morning it was Chuchu who telephoned me.

'What happened last night to change our plans?'

He said he had been a bit drunk and could remember nothing.

'And this Frenchman they want to send with me?'

A Frenchman? He knew nothing about a Frenchman. The General proposed to send me that day in a special plane with a woman who had once been a consul in the United States. I had met her during the boring lunch at the yucca farm in 1976 and had particularly disliked her.

'I won't go to Belize with her. I'll go back to Europe.'

'The General will be disappointed. He wants you very much to go to Belize.'

'All right. Then we'll go on a commercial flight, but it's too late today, and I have to meet García Márquez at the airport.'

We took García Márquez to the Señorial to taste Flor's rum punches, and Márquez telephoned to the Cuban Ambassador who invited all three of us to lunch with him at the Pez de Oro – it seemed a rather unsuitable restaurant for a Communist ambassador to choose, and in fact he never turned up. We waited for more than an hour and then García Márquez and I tossed up to see who would pay for lunch and I won. Meanwhile Chuchu had telephoned the General – sometimes I thought of Panama City as one vast tangle of telephone lines and a medley of contradicting voices. The General, Chuchu told me, had said that Price had been expecting us that day in Belize.

'What about that woman, the ex-consul?'

'He said nothing about her. Anyway, it's too late to do anything today.'

On the way home I saw a soldier leading a tiger – or was it a leopard? – on a chain. A mascot of the Tigers?

We didn't get away next day either, because I was supposed to be meeting some opposition students in a café, but they, like the Cuban Ambassador, never turned up. They probably distrusted me as they knew I was a friend of Omar's. Only the Ultra with the drooping moustache called Juan arrived unexpectedly with his nice wife, and Chuchu presently joined us. I learnt that Juan, like Rogelio and Chuchu, was a mathematics professor. I seemed surrounded by mathematicians. We had a bad lunch at a Chinese restaurant after bad rum punches at the Holiday Inn where an American naval officer was celebrating all by himself the fact that he had become a great-grandfather. The flight to Belize, Chuchu told me, was settled, but we had to leave very early, and remembering our failure to catch the army plane to Managua I made the Ultra's wife promise to wake Chuchu.

She didn't fail me. At 5.15 she drove me and Chuchu to the airport. It proved a slow trek to Belize, with halts at Managua, San José and San Salvador, where the tarmac seemed chock-a-block with fighter planes. I was a little uneasy, as Chuchu had discovered just before we got on the plane that his passport was two years out of date and he had no visa for Belize. However, we were on a mission from the General, and so all was well.

We were met and driven into the city which, poor as it is, had an odd beguiling charm, with wooden houses standing on piles seven feet high above the wet streets and mangrove swamps all around. Perhaps the charm comes from a sense of the temporary, of the precarious, of living on the edge of destruction. The threat is not only from Guatemala, the threat too is from the sea, which seems to be steadily, quietly seeping in, like some guerrilla force which one day will take over the city as it nearly did in 1961 when Hurricane Hattie struck with a tidal wave ten feet high.

The hurricane season was approaching and there were posters on the walls reminiscent of the Blitz days in London and of Kurt Weill's opera, *The Rise and Fall of the City of Mahagonny*.

Hurricane Precautions, 1978

ADVICE TO THE GENERAL PUBLIC
BELIZE CITY

PHASE I
1 Red Flag – *Preliminary warning*

A long list of names was given for the hurricane season, most of them oddly unattractive – who chooses them, I wonder? For this season there were Amelia, Bess, Cora, Debra, Ella, Flossie, Greta, Hope, Irma, Juliet, Kendra, Louise, Martha, Noreen, Ora, Paula, Rosalie, Susan, Tanya, Vanessa, Wanda. I felt glad that my stay was a very short one. Only Amelia could possibly concern me: I wouldn't have to wait until Vanessa and Wanda had passed safely by.

I began to understand, or so I thought, the reason for Omar's affection for George Price and his menaced city. It was as though Belize formed an essential part of the world Omar Torrijos had chosen to live in, a world of confrontation with superior powers, of the dangers and uncertainties of what the next day would bring: in the case of Belize an invasion from Guatemala or a hurricane from the Atlantic. The sole certainty from one day to another was what we had for lunch – a shrimp salad, the only edible form of food we were able to find in Belize.

After the shrimps were finished we were driven out to Belmopan, the new administrative capital which had been built outside the hurricane zone. It reminded me of a tiny Brasilia, and like Brasilia doomed one day to be as dead as Washington without the beauty.

In his office Price seemed to me a shy, reserved man with the touch of uneasy humility one often finds in priests, as though they are always questioning the reality of their own sincerity, but on the long drive which followed in an old Land Rover – his only car – he began to talk obsessively, like a man who has been starved of self-expression for a long time, of theology, literature, his own life. He shared my interest in the Jesuit Teilhard de Chardin, who had been silenced by our Church, and Hans Küng, and my admiration for Thomas Mann. We even shared our preference for *Lotte in Weimar* above *The Magic Mountain*.

He drove us towards the Guatemalan frontier, past the Mennonite farms, where we saw stern, closed German faces, no freedom of women there, no intermarriages, and we stopped at the great Mayan ruins of Xunantunich, where Chuchu tried, but this time vainly, to communicate with his ancestors. We left him alone for a while, throwing strange noises against the great unresponsive stones.

Price said, 'I wrote to you once some years ago.'

I tried to remember for what possible reason the Prime Minister of Belize could have communicated with me, but my memory was as silent as the Mayan temples.

'I asked you what was in *The Over-night Bag*.'

The Over-night Bag was the title of a short story which I had written many years before. I was ashamed to think of how many such letters I had dropped into the waste-paper basket unanswered, so that I was relieved when Price said, 'I was so pleased to get a reply.'

'What did I say?'

'You wrote that there was nothing in the bag.'

I supposed it was the exotic address of Belize which had induced me to reply, for the name George Price could have meant nothing to me then. More than ten years had to pass before I found myself involved by Omar in Central American politics. It was strange to think how a trivial reply like that had won me a friend, for in the course of that drive to the Guatemalan frontier and back I felt I had gained his friendship.

I value that friendship, for he is one of the most interesting political leaders in the world today, governing a parish of about 140,000 inhabitants, made up of Creoles, Germans, Mayan Indians, Black Caribs, Arabs, Chinese and Spanish-speaking refugees from Guatemala.

I write 'a parish', for it is thus, I believe, that George Price thinks of Belize. Price is a Roman Catholic in religion and a socialist in politics – which he never meant to enter. It was his ambition to be a priest. After school he entered a seminary and only abandoned his studies there because his father died and left a large family for whom he had to provide. He still lives as a priest might live, celibate, in one of the small houses set on piles in Belize City. He returns there from Belmopan every evening and goes to bed around nine at latest, for he rises early at 5.30 in the morning for Mass and his daily Communion, and at 8.30 he is back at his desk in the new capital. He told me of the same dream which he had earlier recounted to V. S. Naipaul when Naipaul visited Belize: how in his sleep he had watched with envy and indignation a priest whom he knew to be an old reprobate saying the Mass and consecrating the Host – a rite which was forbidden to him.

As we drove across Belize I was reminded again and again of the priest who lived in the heart of Price. His handwave closely resembled a blessing and he would stop the old Land Rover whenever he was asked for a lift by an Indian or a black. He was the very opposite of the Mennonite farmers who watched us go by with a glum disapproval of our infidel ways.

At the frontier one defiant sign in Spanish of Belize independence – *'Belice Soberano Independiente'* – faced another Guatemalan sign in English, 'Belize is Guatemala.' It amused Price to walk over the frontier with me into the Guatemalan custom house and have a chat with the officials who welcomed him like an old friend.

On the way home we passed by Orange Walk Town, little more than a village, but it possesses a cinema and more than one hotel and Price was planning an international film festival

126

to take place there because it was safely out of the hurricane belt. He told me that he intended to invite world-famous film stars to attend, but I doubt whether this dream of his ever became a reality. I found myself picturing the stars as they sat grandly down to a shrimp meal before attending the cinema which perhaps had seats for two hundred.

At the ford over the New River a peasant stopped us to explain that he had a bad reception on his radio and Price took a note. He took many such notes, and in between we returned to the subject of Hans Küng on infallibility and Thomas Mann's treatment of Goethe.

That night in Belize City Chuchu and I had a bad dinner of shrimps in a small café over the waterfront and we listened to the angry shouts of a black speaker in the street below. We thought at first that it was a political meeting of the Conservative opposition – we had seen them driving around town in jeeps decorated with Union Jacks – but we were wrong. This was a religious meeting and the speaker was declaiming his views on family morality and how errant husbands were the curse of Belize. He seemed a continent away from the sophistication of Panama.

But next day in the local pages of the press the world broke in – there had been an attempted *coup* in Nicaragua, twelve officers of the National Guard had been arrested and more than a hundred civilians. Somoza was threatening to shoot strikers, and the *Reporter*, the opposition paper of Belize, wrote of a 'so-called writer called Green' who had been sent by the Communist Torrijos to see his fellow-Communist Price for reasons which were unknown and certainly sinister.

Chuchu and I read the account of our mission after returning from Corozal, a little town in the north near the Mexican frontier. Price had told me how Doctor Owen, then the British Foreign Secretary, and the British High Commissioner in Belize were anxious to negotiate a settlement with Guatemala by offering the surrender of a slice of land leading to the sea. 'How can a small country of 140,000 inhabitants "negotiate"?' he demanded. 'We can only fight or surrender.' If they let Guatemala have a piece of the cake Mexico would certainly demand a share too, there at Corozal, and little would be left of Belize. Rumours, often without foundation, of off-shore oil only increased the danger.

The day after Chuchu and I were due to leave for Costa Rica, where Chuchu had a rendezvous with a leading Sandinista. Before we left we sat in at the Prime Minister's weekly clinic in Belize City and heard him deal with the problems of his constituents. An old peasant woman complained bitterly of a leaking house which was beyond repair, and a policeman was called in who supported her story. Price promised her immediate redress and she clapped her hands and said she would hold a party in the new house to celebrate.

Before going to the airport we had a typical Belize lunch – no choice except that between shrimps and hamburgers – and it was carelessness or Chuchu's Devil, not the alcohol, that led us, for the second time in my life, to take the wrong plane, so that we found ourselves grounded in San Salvador with hours to wait for a connection. We waited with what particular patience we could muster – nothing would have induced us to leave the safety of the airport, and I prayed that Chuchu's face was strange to those around us and his connection with the Sandinista rebels unknown.

Chuchu despised Costa Rica, the only Central American state without an army, though it was very conveniently situated for his clandestine activities, and he had several times delivered arms to the Sandinistas on its border with Nicaragua with the help of his second-hand plane. He was even irritated, I think, by the ease and safety of his operations. All the same he had been anxious for a long time to show me Costa Rica, in order that I might understand and share his contempt.

I certainly found San José a dreary city under the soaking rain and I was impatient with one of Chuchu's dubious contacts who insisted on leading us away from our hotel to a small restaurant of his choice on the other side of the city where we sat down wet through to a meal quite as bad as any in Belize. The Switzerland of Central America, Costa Rica has often been called – a libel on Switzerland.

Next morning Chuchu made his contact in a café with a tall, dark, serious man, who arrived with a very attractive girl whom I seemed to remember having encountered the year before in the Pigeon House with other refugees. The girl and I made small talk at a table far enough away from Chuchu and his companion for me not to catch any word of their discussion. I was to meet them again more than four years later in Managua – Comandante Daniel Ortega, the leading member of the Nicaraguan Junta, and his wife, Rosario.

That afternoon we went back to Panama and two days later, after reporting to Omar on our visit to Belize, there was another last farewell to Chuchu at the airport before I took the KLM plane to Amsterdam. In the last meeting with the General there had been nothing really to report – except my liking for Price and my dislike of his Conservative enemies with their wild accusations, their violent opposition to independence and their fake Union Jack loyalty.

One of the endearing qualities of Omar was his desire to hear what others thought of the characters with whom he dealt. He was not offended by my suspicion of his Chief of Staff, Colonel Flores – he simply took it into account. Indeed, he had an exaggerated respect for that instinct for human character which is perhaps inherent in an imaginative writer, and he was reassured when García Márquez or myself liked the same man or woman whom he liked. 'What do you think of so and so?' was a question which came easily to his lips. He was loyal to his friends – to Tito whom he regarded as a father figure, to Fidel Castro who had fought the sort of war he had longed to fight himself – and his opinion would not be altered by anything we might say, but he was happy if our opinion coincided with his own. So he was happy that I liked George Price, and perhaps it was the only reason that he had sent us to Belize – in order that one friend might meet another.

PART IV

1979 and 1980

1

In 1979 the civil war in Nicaragua drew to an end, Somoza was defeated and fled the country, and the Sandinistas were at last in power. There was no reason why the telephone should ever sound again with a call summoning me to Panama.

However much I felt the loss of my friendship for Omar and Chuchu, there were good reasons for me to stay at home in France: in March I was in hospital having part of my intestines removed, and almost simultaneously events broke out in the private life of myself and my friends that led eventually to my writing a pamphlet called *J'Accuse*.

The battlefield for me was now in France, not in Central America; the fight was on behalf of a young mother, the daughter of my greatest friend, and her two small children. Violence was on my own doorstep and not far away across a frontier, and I had no time to worry about the politics of Central America. For months too after my operation I was a tired man who had to ration what strength he had, and I couldn't have faced the long flight to Panama.

All the same if one takes a side, one takes a side, come what may. I wasn't to escape my involvement as easily as that. I couldn't go to Panama, but it was Panama which came again to me. At one o'clock in the morning on the last day of April, the telephone woke me from sleep, and it was Chuchu's voice which spoke to me. 'Graham, I thought you were not there.'

'I was fast asleep, Chuchu. Where are you?'

'In Panama, of course. I have a message for you from the General. He is sending someone to see you. He will arrive in Antibes during the next few days. The General very much wants you to talk to him.'

'Which day will he arrive?'

'I don't know that. He has left Panama. Now he is in Mexico, I think. Yesterday the General asked when you were coming to Panama.'

'I can't, Chuchu. Not this year. I have been ill, and I have troubles here. I can't get away.'

'But you'll see the messenger?'

'Of course.'

Two days later, as I was preparing for bed, the telephone rang again. A voice told me that the speaker had a message for me from the General, and I made an appointment with him for the next morning. When he arrived, I recognized him as a young man whom I had seen once before in Omar's company. He asked me whether I had read in the papers a month or so back of the kidnapping of two English bankers by the guerrillas in El Salvador.

'Yes. I remember.'

'The General is afraid they are in danger of death. The bank seems to have lost all contact with the guerrillas. He wants you to talk to their head office in London and tell them that the guerrillas are prepared to drop two of their conditions – the first that six of their number must be released from prison. They are sure now that the men are dead. The second condition they are ready to drop too. About a communiqué to be published in the local and the world press. Only the third is left – a matter of money. You mustn't tell the bank the source of your information.'

'But which bank?'

'The Bank of London.'

I had heard of the Bank of England but not of the Bank of London. 'Are you sure of the name?'

'Yes, yes. The matter is very urgent.'

I had never been more thankful for my copy of Whitaker's *Almanack*. With its help I identified the bank he referred to as the Bank of London and Montreal, a branch of Lloyds International, with headquarters in Nassau. All the same I felt myself out of depth in this world of banking.

'Will you come back at 6.30 and dine with me?'

I remembered that my nephew Graham, the Managing Director of Jonathan Cape, belonged to the banking branch of the Guinness family and on his advice I found myself talking to a Mr W, who was dealing with the kidnapping affair. It was an embarrassing and hesitant conversation.

'How do you know all this?'

'I have a very reliable source, but I am not allowed to give you his name.'

The silence on the line seemed charged with very reasonable suspicion. My home in Antibes and my profession as a novelist must have seemed to Mr W strangely remote from an affair of kidnapping in El Salvador.

I tried to sound more convincing. 'You see, during the last three years I have been spending quite a lot of time in Central America. I have had a good many contacts.'

'Why do you think they are dropping these conditions?'

'I think perhaps they don't want to kill the men.'

The rather dry voice of Mr W replied, 'That has been our impression, too.'

'I understand that you have lost contact with the guerrillas?'

'Yes.'

'I have been given a telephone number in Mexico City. If you will ring it . . .'

When the young man returned that evening I told him what had passed. He raised both hands in the air and said with satisfaction, '*Mission accomplie.*'

'Would you like to telephone Panama?'

'No, but if you don't mind I will telephone Mexico.'

A few moments later he dropped the receiver and said, 'The bank has already made contact.'

At dinner I suggested that we should meet next morning before he took his plane home and I would show him the old town of Antibes. He agreed, but he never turned up. I rang his hotel, but he was already on his way back to Central America, and a few weeks later the bankers were released. For some while I nursed a greedy hope that I might perhaps receive in return for the mysterious telephone number at least a case of whisky from Lloyds International, but the hope soon faded. Probably the directors thought I had received from the guerrillas a commission on the five-million-dollar ransom which I believe they paid.

I don't know how or when I happened to learn the name of the contact in Mexico City – it was that of my friend Gabriel García Márquez. García Márquez, it seemed, was trying to organize a Central American equivalent to Amnesty International.

I was busy all that year with my private war and I was finishing with difficulty a short novel, *Doctor Fischer of Geneva*, so when the summer came and Chuchu was again on the telephone asking me when I would be arriving ('The General wants to know'), I could only answer, 'Not this year. I told you it's impossible. Of course I want to come. Perhaps next year . . .'

2

It was in January 1980, again as I was preparing for bed, that the telephone rang and a woman's voice said, 'Mr Shearer wants to speak to you.' I was sleepy and I thought the name resembled that of a film producer whom I had once known, but it was a stranger's voice which came on the line.

'Mr Greene?'

'Yes, but excuse me – who are you, Mr Shearer?'

'I am the South African Chargé d'Affaires in Paris. We thought you might be able to help us.'

'Help you?'

'Perhaps you have read in the newspapers that our Ambassador, Mr Dunne, was kidnapped in El Salvador some months ago. We haven't been able to contact the kidnappers. We thought perhaps that you might be able to help us.'

'Help you?' I repeated. It almost seemed at that moment

136

as though Antibes had become a small island anchored off the coast of central America and involved in all the problems there.

I said, 'There *is* a telephone number in Mexico City, but I haven't got it any more. I destroyed it. Perhaps if you could speak to Mr W at Lloyds International . . . I once gave him the number and he may have kept it.' Half an hour later Mr Shearer rang again and provided the number, so that further action on my part was required.

It was some days before I was able to get García Márquez on the telephone. He said, 'A *South African* Ambassador? That's a bit more of a problem.'

'This is a human question not a political one. I understand he's a sick man and his wife is dying of cancer.' (I had been talking again to Mr Shearer.)

'We have to find out first which of five guerrilla groups hold him.'

More days passed and Márquez was again on the line. 'It seems to be the FPL. But it would be much better if the family made the contact – not the South African Government. For obvious reasons.'

I passed the news to Mr Shearer who said that he would pass it on to Pretoria. 'But there are difficulties,' he told me. 'The wife is dying, the son is a bit of a hippy, there's only the daughter and she's a young girl.'

'Can't someone pretend to be one of the family?'

I heard no more for a long while, but on 18 August (I had given way to Chuchu's pressure) I set off yet again for Panama at 10.30 in the evening after spending eight hours in the Van Gogh lounge at Amsterdam airport, a lounge in which I had begun to feel very much at home. Before I left I had written to Mr Shearer, asking him whether I could be of any further use to him when I was in Panama, but he had replied that the affair was now in the hands of Washington. Contact had been made with the guerrillas, and it would be better for me not to cross lines.

137

Chuchu was there next morning at the Panama airport. He had grown a beard, but was otherwise unchanged in the two years which had passed, and he bubbled over with news. The General, it seemed, wanted me to go to Nicaragua in two days' time, and this suited Chuchu well, for the two of his children whom I had already encountered were now in Nicaragua, deposited by their mother. The girl was at school and anxious to join the army and her young brother had become a guard to Tomás Borge and had shot himself accidentally in the leg.

As usual in Panama our plans were soon upset by the innumerable telephone conversations that took place between our rum punches, which as usual were badly made and expensive. The Señorial to our distress had been turned into yet another bank and we searched in vain for the young woman Flor on whose rum punches we had always been able to rely. Banks in Panama City grew as quickly as weeds in a garden. There were now about a hundred and thirty of them, a rather strange situation in a country under a social democratic leader. My visit to Nicaragua in any case would have to be postponed because the FPL guerrilla leader, Salvador Cayetano, who went under the code-name of Marcial, was in Panama City and wanted to see me.

There was other more personal news – Chuchu had got married yet again, this time to the sister of Lidia, the wife of Rogelio the Sandinista, and he had had a baby. The General too had a new baby – with the girl whom I had met two years back. After the birth he had told Chuchu that he should also make a baby, and Chuchu, the faithful bodyguard, promptly obeyed.

Chuchu was less happy about another of the General's romantic notions – to rescue Señora Perón from her house arrest in Argentina. He introduced me to her lawyer from Buenos Aires whom Chuchu didn't trust at all, and we went together to see the Vice-President, Ricardo de la Espriella, who promptly wrote out a cheque for $20,000 which Chuchu cashed at a bank and handed the cash to the lawyer. 'That's the last we'll see of him,' he said. The General's idea was that the money would go to bribe her guards to look the other way while she escaped to an airport where a Panamanian plane would be awaiting her. Months later she was released by the Argentinian Junta in quite a normal fashion and set off to Madrid, so perhaps the money ended up as Chuchu had foreseen.

Bernard Diederich was back in Panama, and as Chuchu was fully occupied sitting beside the telephone as he waited for the General to call, we took his car and drove into what three years ago had been the Canal Zone. There was little sign of any change except that now the Panamanian flag flew over Ancón Hill and the offices of the Canal Company. We drank good rum punches and ate a terrible Irish stew at the American Legion Club with a New Zealand friend of Diederich – a very enigmatic man who avoided answering any direct questions. I was not sure whether he was afraid of the correspondent of *Time* or of me.

That night I had supper with the General. His girl was there and Omar introduced his baby with pride – a daughter. 'When I can communicate with her,' he joked to his girl, 'I won't need you.' There was some heavy drinking. Boyd, the former Foreign Minister, was there, and a poet whose name I never caught. Never before had I felt so strong an impression of Omar as a lonely man, a man genuinely affectionate, who grasped at friendship as greedily as he grasped at books, as though there were too little time left for him to catch up on either. At one moment he rebuked me with anger when I slipped into formality because of a stranger's presence, 'I don't like it when you call me General and not Omar.' He asked me how I had liked the Vice-President. 'Very much,' I said and he looked relieved. I think perhaps he was remembering my reaction to Colonel Flores.

Chuchu, Diederich and I should have left the next day for Nicaragua as guests of Tomás Borge, but first I had to see the El

Salvador guerrilla leader, Marcial. The General explained that Marcial was in Panama for a conference between the five guerrilla groups to plan what they believed then would be the final offensive.

Marcial came to my hotel with a young G-2 officer. He was a very small elderly man in glasses with tiny twitching hands and tiny feet. If there was something merciless in his eyes, this was understandable – he had a long personal history behind him of imprisonment and torture. Almost at once he admitted that his real name was Cayetano and he suggested that we should move into the bedroom, leaving the G-2 officer behind. Seated on my bed he came directly to the point. 'I understand from Mexico that you are interested in the fate of the South African Ambassador.'

I was aware of how weak my cards were. 'For humanitarian reasons,' I said. 'His wife is dying of cancer.' I had already played these cards too often on the telephone to Mexico to have any confidence in them. He listened, however, with courtesy, and afterwards there was a long embarrassing silence while I tried to think of just one more card I might play and failed to find it. It was a relief when he spoke. He assured me that everything was going, as he put it, all right, and there were only a few small details left to be arranged – the ransom, for example. I suggested the names of two South African millionaires who might be prepared to help. He had not heard of them and made a note. He was becoming more human every moment: he gave me an occasional smile and I thought that I detected a gleam of friendship in what had seemed his cold eyes. He told me he had four friends down below and I remembered that there were five guerrilla groups in El Salvador. Could he ask them to come up and speak to me? I agreed and we rejoined the G-2 officer in the sitting-room.

All four turned out to be young men, and Cayetano called on one of them to speak to me in English. He spoke very dully and at great length: a propagandist exercise. When it was over I asked them about the killing of certain peasants. I said that in the eyes of the West these killings, which had been reported in the press, had injured their cause. Cayetano replied, 'In such cases you must put the word "peasant" in inverted commas. They were informers.'

My thoughts were with the kidnapped man. I tried to think of some way to help him. If they could be made to believe that I might be of some use to them, then perhaps . . . Rather unconvincingly I suggested that they suffered from 'disinformation' supplied by their enemies to the European press: if they would send me accurate information, not propaganda, I would try to have it published. With that we parted. I received no news from them, the final offensive failed to be final, and months later confirmation came to Europe of the Ambassador's death. He was a sick man and he had been dragged here and there as a hostage for months. Mr Shearer wrote to me from Pretoria: 'We are inclined on balance to think he was not "executed" as claimed by FMNL [the organization of all five guerrilla groups], but that he died as naturally as possible in the circumstances. There is, of course, no proof. The body and its whereabouts have never been revealed.' Two years were to pass before I saw Cayetano again and then the meeting was in Nicaragua on the eve of his own mysterious death.

4

Next day Chuchu, Diederich and I flew in Omar's private jet to Managua. He was determined to continue my education for better or worse, and for that reason he had arranged the invitation from Tomás Borge.

Managua is an almost non-existent city without any centre, the whole centre having been destroyed by the earthquake which so enriched President Somoza, for he pocketed all the international aid which was sent to Nicaragua instead of squandering it on rebuilding the capital. In the centre of the former city there remain only the cathedral which is half in ruins, the Inter-Continental Hotel, a small Mexican restaurant, the National Palace which had been seized by Eden Pastora, and the Bunker where Somoza had spent his last days of the presidency under fire. Life existed only on the periphery of Managua, so that to visit anyone there involved a drive of nearly half an hour.

We were due to arrive on a day of great importance. In an attempt to improve the illiteracy rate of fifty per cent the Sandinista government had despatched five thousand school-children from the upper forms to live and work with the peasants in the country for six months, and in the evening to teach them reading and writing. There had been casualties. About fifty children had died from disease and seven had been murdered by the remnants of Somoza's National Guard who were operating as guerrillas from the safety of Honduras, but the result of the exercise was spectacular – the illiteracy rate, it was claimed, had been reduced from fifty per cent to thirteen per cent. On this day the children were to return to a public welcome, which was to be spectacular too. The earthquake had fashioned a vast open-air theatre capable of holding 600,000 spectators – standing room only, of course.

It was explained to our little party that the Inter-Continental Hotel was full of visitors for the occasion and we were driven to a very comfortable house beyond the periphery with two charming and pretty maids to look after us. We had been welcomed at the airport – to Chuchu's dissatisfaction – by María Isabel who, separated now from Camilo, had become an assistant to Tomás Borge and in her military uniform looked even prettier than two years ago. Our maids served us a simple and excellent lunch, but I felt disgruntled, for I believed myself to be separated from what I mistakenly thought to be the centre of things. I had not realized the emptiness of that centre. Indeed, I was quite unfairly suspicious, feeling that there must be a purpose in this separation, which I was ready to regard as a luxurious house arrest. However, to comfort me Diederich telephoned to the manager of the Inter-Continental, whom he knew well from civil war days, and arranged our transfer there for the next morning when the spectacular would be over and the visitors gone. I felt happier to think that we would be paying for our own rooms and be no charge on the Sandinistas. After lunch we drove back to Managua.

We had seats on the platform at the sunny end and the heat was blistering. But the heat seemed not to have deterred the enormous crowd below who had hardly elbow room. On the platform were ministers of government, members of the Junta, the President of Costa Rica. The schoolchildren marched below to shattering applause, each group with its own banner, and afterwards we had to suffer three hours of speeches. A successful revolution seems always to be marked by long speeches, just as war is marked by long periods of waiting for action.

The President of Costa Rica spoke first. Like a good social democrat he pleaded earnestly for early elections. Those on the platform listened to him in a glum, disapproving silence, and so did the crowd below. There was no sign of enthusiasm. After a victory in arms against heroic odds 'early elections' is not a rousing slogan in Central America. Another outsider spoke next – the Bishop of Cuernavaca, popularly known in Mexico as the Red Bishop. He too failed to arouse interest. Then came the army leader and Minister of Defence, Humberto Ortega. He began by proclaiming frankly that there would be no elections before 1985, and these words were greeted with enthusiasm by the packed crowd below and even stronger enthusiasm by the middle-class types on the platform who were thus able to show their disapproval of the President of Costa Rica. It was as though the men on the platform were reassuring the crowd of their loyalty by their applause and the crowd cheered them back, reassuring them in return. 'No elections before 1985' – that was a revolutionary slogan which they could understand.

I was puzzled by their response until I remembered what the word 'elections' meant in Nicaragua. During his long reign Somoza had frequently called elections and had thus legitimized his dictatorship, if only in the eyes of the United States, by winning all of them with huge majorities. So 'election' for most people in the crowd was a word which meant trickery. 'No elections' was a promise to them of no trickery.

After that popular beginning Ortega spoke for too long. His speech lasted more than an hour, and he was no Castro. He lost the attention of the crowd. They began to move restlessly around and a murmur of innumerable conversations rose towards the platform. One could watch the crowd thinning. Many were struggling out to go home. Then the small intense figure of Tomás Borge took Ortega's place, the crowd sprang to attention, all faces turned again to the platform, the murmur ceased. He spoke only for five minutes, but he was speaking to an audience who listened to every word.

The sun was unbearably hot. A small cloud which promised rain came and went. We decided to wait for only one more speaker. She was worth waiting for – a peasant woman of middle age. She was one of those who had been taught to read and write by the schoolchildren in their crusade against illiteracy, and now she read out to the huge hushed audience something she had composed, and that something was a poem. Nicaragua, I remembered Chuchu telling me, was a country of poets.

Down below the platform we found Chuchu's children: the boy was still limping after the accident with his rifle, and the girl argued fiercely with her father about her wish to leave school and join the army.

There too, wandering alone – he had not been visible on the platform among the chiefs of the revolution – was the hero who had captured the National Palace, Eden Pastora, or Commandant Cero as he had been called when I met him in Panama after inheriting the title from Camilo's brother. His handsome actor's face gave an impression of loneliness, sadness, disappointment. I was not surprised when I heard a year later that he had turned against the Sandinistas and gone into exile. He had achieved the most spectacular feat of the civil war, and now he was in charge of training the local militia. An

144

honourable situation, but can an actor who has once played Henry V to the world's applause be content afterwards with the part of Pistol?

Next year he left the country claiming that he would never fight against his late companions; and after that he wandered restlessly from Panama to Mexico, from Mexico to Costa Rica. Supported by whom? Perhaps by certain characters in Miami, the Valley of the Fallen, or by the CIA. His promise was later modified – though he rejected the Sandinista government he would never fight on the side of the Somozistas, and that promise I can well believe that he intended to keep. The scent of glory was still in his nostrils – the sense of battling against great odds with a few chosen companions, and now, as I write, he is said to have formed a commando of about five hundred men across the frontier of Costa Rica on Nicaraguan soil with which to defeat his former comrades. His commando will certainly prove a dangerous nuisance, but if they succeed it will inevitably be as a small unit fighting with the United States, the El Salvador death squads, the Honduran army, and the men in Miami against the same enemy.

Pastora is a tragic figure. With his courage and charisma (a dangerous quality when a man becomes conscious of possessing it) he has been doomed to disillusion. If the Marxist Left should be defeated, he will inevitably fall out with the conservatives and the capitalists who find him useful now, and who will afterwards despise him for his simplicity and even his heroism. I find myself still haunted two years later by the memory of that solitary man wandering along alone below the platform where all the other leaders sat facing the enormous crowd who had come to welcome what he as much as any man had helped to bring about.*

* As a slow writer I find it difficult to keep up with the changing events in Central America. Even a footnote written in November 1983 will probably be out of date when this book is published. Pastora proved for a time to be a more dangerous figure than I thought. After establishing his headquarters in Nicaragua close to the Costa Rican border he even acquired some small planes. One was shot down over Managua where it was trying to bomb the home of the Foreign

145

After the parade, the speeches, the crowd, the enthusiasm, it was odd to find myself drinking whisky that evening in a rich bourgeois home belonging to a member of the Chamorro family, who owned the conservative newspaper *La Prensa*. *La Prensa* would soon become a strong opponent of the Sandinista government, but the Chamorro family, as so often happens in civil war, was divided, and Xavier Chamorro, in whose house Tomás Borge had made a rendezvous to meet and talk with me, was editor of *El Nuevo Diario*, a pro-Sandinista paper. All the same, it seemed strange to meet the leading Marxist in such very un-Marxist surroundings. Perhaps he felt as ill at ease as myself, but polarization had not yet fully set in – for the moment the Sandinistas' victory was welcomed by almost the whole country. The future was only hinted at in the sad eyes of the neglected hero below the platform.

This was a brief, only too touristic visit to a country struggling back to normal life after a long civil war, yet I had no desire to stay longer. My personal problems in France called me back. Next day, after booking in at the Inter-Continental Hotel, we drove to the small town of Masaya which had been the scene of some of the fiercest fighting and which still bore the scars, then on to the beautiful city of Granada – a very conservative city – where Chuchu had a fierce interchange with an intrusive journalist from *La Prensa*.

The days in Nicaragua equalled the days in Panama for frustrations and delays. We had planned to return to Panama on a certain day, and it was lucky that we checked and found that María Isabel had somehow managed to book us on a flight which didn't exist – we were not to be much luckier with the flight to which she changed us. In order to pass the time we drove to León, a less beautiful city than Granada, and up to the

Minister, Father D'Escoto, and another bombed the small Pacific port of Corinto. But then, clinging to the last shreds of his promise, he refused the demand of the CIA that in return for their support he should join the main counter-revolutionary organization which contained members of the old Somoza National Guard, and he withdrew – for how long? – from the scene of action.

fort above the city where Somoza's men had been besieged, and we visited a small tradesman's house where a Sandinista supporter showed us where he had successfully kept arms concealed from the National Guard under the false floor of a wardrobe.

Back in Managua, we chose badly for dinner – at a restaurant called Los Ranchos which served poor and expensive food with a false elegance. Here my sympathies for the Sandinistas became strengthened, for I felt myself surrounded by their opponents, men in ties and waistcoats who had dressed up in spite of the heat for an evening out and who regarded our open shirts with a suspicion shared by the waiters who deliberately delayed our meals. Here we were on enemy territory, and I was glad to get away as soon as the bill could be prepared.

We were up early next day because we were uncertain of our seats on a Panamanian plane since María Isabel had performed a second difficult feat of getting us tickets but no reservations. The plane was there all right, but there was an indefinite and unexplained delay in boarding. Tomás Borge arrived with an armed escort to say goodbye and he wanted photographs of the occasion, but my camera had been stolen from my hotel room (a great relief to me, for it rid me of the responsibility of taking photographs, though I regretted the loss of some rather good pictures of vultures in Panama City). However, Tomás Borge had the necessary authority to borrow a camera from a duty free shop, so that I have a record of our affectionate farewell.

Finally we succeeded in getting on the plane, the plane began to move down the tarmac, and suddenly there was nothing to be seen through the windows but smoke. The plane stopped abruptly and we got out. We were told, as it proved untruly, that the plane would not leave that day. It was ten o'clock in the morning. The only other plane was Salvadorean and would not leave until six in the evening. We transferred our reservations to it. I went on a half-hearted search for my camera (luckily unsuccessful), and after lunch at the hotel we drove up to the

147

volcano which dominates Managua, into which Somoza is said to have dropped the bodies of some of his opponents. A thin trail of smoke like that from a crematorium coiled up towards us from the crater and down below in the heart of the crater itself dozens of parakeets flew here and there like coloured kites manoeuvred by an unseen hand. I was sad to leave them to return to the airport, where nothing seemed to go right. It was 4.30. The Panamanian flight after all had left at three, and the Salvador plane, it was said, would be forty minutes late. That proved to be an optimistic reckoning – later it was announced that the plane had not even left Miami and might not arrive at all.

Politics can be a distraction from boredom, and politics entered the lounge now in the person of a distinguished black in a Mao suit who was followed by a wife – or secretary or mistress? – and a retainer. He took his seat firmly beside us, leaving his companions on two less comfortable chairs behind him, and silence descended after an initial greeting. I felt we were suspect – perhaps because I was an Englishman, an ex-colonialist. For how long, I wondered, were we to be condemned to this aggressive silence?

I remembered the bottle of whisky which I always carried in my handbag, and I suggested that since we had an indefinite wait ahead of us, we might ask for some water and broach the bottle. The stranger accepted for himself, though he refused for his companions, and the whisky had an immediate effect. Volubility succeeded silence. He had been visiting Nicaragua as the representative of Mr Bishop and the Grenada government. A stream of Marxist clichés came pouring out of him with his life story. He was a lawyer and he had taken his law degree in Dublin (it was hard to picture him walking on the banks of the Liffey or sitting in an Irish pub). Afterwards he was called to the Bar in London. He asked my name and said that he had been made to read some of my books at school. After a second whisky he invited me to come as a guest of his government to Grenada, and I asked for a rain check. I described him later to

148

Omar. 'Ah,' he said, 'I know the man. He's to the right of the President, and a good deal to the left of me.'

In the end the plane did turn up from Miami and it contained the Canadian Archbishop of Panama. 'For God's sake, let's avoid him,' I said to Chuchu, but there was no danger of his seeing us. Immediately on landing the Archbishop dived into the duty free liquor store, open to arriving passengers as well as departing, while we preserved our thirst for a little shabby Jamaican restaurant to which we had become attached, the Montego Bay, kept by an old jovial black, whose rum punches were almost as good as Flor's. Drinking them, I had the usual thought: 'Well, I've seen a little of Nicaragua, thanks to Omar – a first and a last visit,' and again as always in Central America I was to be proved wrong.

I had begun to distrust the legend that Panamanians only drank at the weekend. Perhaps Chuchu had been corrupted in my company, but when after leaving the Montego Bay we went on to Omar's second home, at the house of Rory González, dinner had not yet started and drinks were going the round with no thought of the weekend to come. Perhaps it was only the peasants who abided by the unwritten rule because of poverty. After dinner the hour was very late. Chuchu had unwisely moved from rum to whisky to wine. One of the General's guards wanted to drive me back, but Chuchu refused to leave the wheel of his car and I felt morally bound to let him take me. Somebody must wisely have summoned his wife, for Silvana arrived suddenly beside the car. Chuchu had not yet grown accustomed to marriage, and he accused her of being wifely.

Sylvana remained beautifully unperturbed. She was twenty-four and he was forty-eight, and she knew that in the long run he was no match for her when it came to obstinacy. Yet he clung to the wheel for a long time and when at last he took his hands away he got out of the car without a word and went back into the house as though he couldn't bear to see the result of his surrender. Silvana smiled as she drove. She knew her Chuchu and was quite sure of him. That too was perhaps an aggravation to Chuchu – that she could be sure of him.

As we drove to the hotel I was again thinking of the novel which was doomed never to be written, *On the Way Back*. I believed that I had discovered what was wrong with it, what was preventing its free growth in my mind. The setting was too closely fixed on Panama – I ought to make the scene an imaginary Central American state. After all, I had seen a little of Nicaragua, a little of Belize. The 'way back' should not bear only a reference to the woman's journey with Chuchu and a way back which never happened – the phrase should have a political meaning too: the failure of a revolution. The villain of the piece must be based on Señor V, the man whom I was in the habit of calling Fish Face to the General – a relic of the Arias regime. I thought of the bourgeois diners in Managua and the surly waiters who were on the side of wealth. They too had small parts to play. Perhaps it ought not to be Chuchu who died at the end of the novel, but the General, who so often dreamed of death. Alas, how true that was to prove in fact!

5

Next day Chuchu had quite recovered when he came to fetch me for lunch with Omar, but he was in some distress because he had lost his dog. It was a singularly stupid dog, as he had often complained to me, and a savage one at that, and it was much hated by his neighbours. Now it had simply walked away and he had spent hours tramping the streets in search of it.

'How I hate dogs,' he said.

'Then why do you keep one?'

'It's the only way to keep my hate within me.'

I told myself, 'Surely this dog has a part to play in *On the Way Back*.'

At lunch that day with Omar I was aware more than ever of the affection which had grown up between us. He even com-

150

pared the friendship he felt for me with the affection he had for Tito before his death. 'Our relationship was a little the same,' he said.

Tito and me – it seemed a strange comparison. I think he meant that his affection was based with both of us on a kind of trust. As I have already written, he always liked to compare his opinion of a character with mine. Poor Fish Face was one example – Omar even adopted my title when he spoke of him. Now he wanted to hear my opinion of Tomás Borge. I told him that at our first meeting in the bourgeois household I hadn't much cared for him, but afterwards when he came out to the airport to speak to me next day my opinion of him had changed completely, perhaps because he was more relaxed. 'Yes,' Omar said, 'for the first few minutes one dislikes him.'

We talked of Mrs Thatcher and her attitude to Belize, which seemed to imply a willingness to negotiate with Guatemala. He wanted me to have another meeting with George Price. The position of Belize was becoming more difficult in relation to its aggressive authoritarian neighbour. Colombia and Venezuela no longer supported her. Panama and Nicaragua were the only countries now on whom Price could rely in the Organization of American States. Price was at the moment in Miami where he was meeting the Foreign Minister of Guatemala – the first direct contact between the two countries. Omar had wanted Chuchu and me to go to Belize – now he wanted to invite Price to Panama and he told Chuchu to telephone him.

One remark of Omar's stayed in my mind (was it perhaps a defence of Mrs Thatcher or a criticism of her?), 'Ignorance can be good in politics. Carter and I agreed about the Canal Treaty because we were both ignorant of the problems it raised. If we hadn't been ignorant the Treaty would never have been signed.'

Next morning Chuchu rang me up to say that he had spoken to Price on the telephone, but Chuchu admitted that he had been a little drunk at the time and he couldn't remember what

Price had said. I felt a little drunk myself later that day after three rum punches at the Montego Bay and three pisco sours at the Peruvian restaurant, from the door of which I saw a number of elephants walking through the rain in the centre of Panama City. First a tiger and now elephants. I am sure it was not the drink that saw them.

With the situation in El Salvador and Nicaragua and the menace to Belize from Guatemala, Panama seemed thicker than ever with political problems and personalities. That night in the house of a Communist there was a party for the Nicaraguan Ambassador, who was being transferred to Cuba. He sat glum and alone at this party in his honour and nobody spoke to him until I did.

Suddenly all our plans were changed. Price was not coming to Panama, nor were we going to Belize: Omar had agreed to my unwise wish: a visit to Bocas del Toro.

6

Chuchu and I took off next day in a small military plane. The weather was very bad – squalls and heavy rain which made visibility almost nil. I was glad Omar was not with us, for this was the kind of weather which he loved to fly in: he would have told the pilot to press on in spite of it. Without him our pilot could show a measure of prudence and we came down at David in the hope of the weather clearing before we took off over the mountains of Chiriquí for the Atlantic coast. While we waited, fear lent me arguments against going on. Why should Chuchu and I not take a car, I argued, and revisit that pretty mountain village of Boquete with its fresh air and its little hotel and the charming hostess who looked like Oona Chaplin? But the pilot had something of Omar's spirit. The weather was a challenge which he had to accept, and after half an hour he decided that it had improved enough for us to fly on.

I could see little sign of improvement, though it was true that now occasionally when the clouds whirled apart we caught a glimpse of the mountain tops and then of the sea boiling below. We landed in a deluge of rain on a small island which seemed to be sinking back into the sea under the weight of the storm. This was the Bocas I had been so determined to visit.

We walked, ankle deep in water, to a little hotel called the Bahía opposite the jetty where the banana boats used to tie up. After one look at the place I was relieved to be told that there was no room available. Apparently in this benighted town an agricultural fair was in progress and there were even visitors who had been prepared to come from the other islands around. Now, I thought with relief, we will surely have to fly back whatever the weather, but while we stood and argued in a sodden group the proprietor returned – he had found one room for us, he said, and what a room it proved to be: two iron bedsteads and a chair were the only furniture. A bare electric globe dangled from the centre of the ceiling, there was no air-conditioning to relieve the damp heat, and no mosquito wire over the windows. I even envied the pilot who was going to return through the storm to Panama. He would fetch us, he told me, the next morning at 9.30. But suppose, I couldn't help wondering, the weather turns even worse and we are stranded for days in this terrible spot . . . An awful lunch in an empty restaurant did nothing to cheer us: a thin soup with two bits of meat floating in it: a scrap of chicken, mainly skin: no rum – only a weak bottled beer.

Well, at least the rain had temporarily stopped, and nothing was left for us to do but to visit the so-called fair in a field on the other side of the island. There was no drainage: the rain just collected where it fell, and to cross a street dry shod meant taking a flying leap.

The fair consisted of a double row of uninteresting stalls – uninteresting to us but obviously quite an event for the inhabitants of Bocas del Toro. They were mainly blacks of West Indian origin and in the medley of voices one could distinguish English, Spanish and Creole. Chuchu ran into a black acquaintance called Raúl who had once been a student of his and we went to a stall and drank bad rum.

Raúl, it appeared, intended to stand as an independent candidate in the elections which were to be held in 1981 and which would be open to political parties as a result of the Canal Treaty. His two opponents represented the Communist Party and the new Government Party founded by Omar. He had a grievance – his constituency consisted of several islands and unlike his rivals he hadn't got the money to hire a boat to visit them: he hadn't even the money to buy the T-shirts which he judged were essential for a successful campaign. We were joined by another man whom Raúl introduced as his manager, but I couldn't understand a word of his English.

The bad rum was working in my bladder, and I went to a smelly little shed to urinate against the wall. A black came in to pee beside me and at once he began to talk. He told me that he was an engineer and that in a few years he was going to retire with a pension and look after his father's big cocoa farm.

We buttoned up side by side, but he made no attempt to leave the shed or stop talking. I said, 'You'll be a rich man then.'

'Not rich, ma'an, but wealthy.'

He went on to tell me that his grandfather had been an Oxford professor. 'You've heard of Oxford, ma'an?'

'Yes.'

Another man came in to pee. He wanted to sell me an old sword. I explained that if I took it on a plane with me I would be arrested as a hijacker. Then the grandson of the Oxford professor cadged the price of a glass of rum from me and I was able to rejoin my friend. Raúl recognized the man when I described him. He said he was known all over Bocas del Toro as the Greatest Liar. He once had the whole police force searching for a crashed plane in the wrong place.

I couldn't drink any more bad rum, so I said I would go back to the hotel. The island seemed to be sinking further into the water and it was beginning to rain again.

A white man with an American accent greeted me on my way

out of the fair. He wanted me to have a drink, but I told him I was going to take a siesta. He said he had a house which was painted blue on the jetty nearly opposite the hotel. 'You can't miss it. Come and have a drink whenever you like,' he said. I began to walk back, but a police car stopped beside me and offered me a lift. 'It would be safer for you,' a policeman explained, and I remembered the police van in Colón.

At the hotel I found that the bare globe in the bedroom didn't work – when the dark came there would be only a reflected light from the bathroom. I lay down and tried in vain to interest myself in Doctorow's *Ragtime* till dusk came and reading was impossible. So was sleep. I lay for an hour on my back and felt an awful nostalgia for my home and my friends in Antibes. In spite of my affection for Omar and Chuchu, Antibes was where my real loyalties lay. I had left my friends to face alone their enemies in Nice. No telegram from them, if they needed help, could reach me in Bocas. I had booked my plane home to leave Panama in a few days' time, but I had a sense of doom in Bocas – a feeling that I would never get away. It was my own fault. I had wanted to see the point where Columbus had turned back. I had wanted to see the place where no tourist went. I had tried twice before and failed. I should have taken the hint which Providence had provided.

Finally in desperation I got up and dressed and crossed the street to the house of the friendly Yankee. 'My name is Eugene,' he greeted me, 'but most people call me Pete.' He had put a skull on either side of the door to frighten away thieves.

After he had poured out two generous whiskies my spirits picked up. He told me he was a pilot on Braniff Airlines and during the war he had been a pilot for the OSS, the American secret service. He had bought sixty-seven acres on the island, plus another house on a beach, for six thousand dollars, and he planned to retire there in two years and keep the acres as a bird and animal sanctuary. His happiness on Bocas astonished me and I looked at him with a new respect. He had no wife or family, but he was soon joined by two lively local women with whom he planned to have a 'riotous evening' at the fair. He invited me to join them, but Chuchu had sent word that he was waiting for me.

We had been invited to dinner, it seemed by Raúl, the parliamentary candidate, at the house of his mother, Veronica, a dynamic woman who spoke perfect English and matched me glass for glass with whisky to which she added coconut milk, as the water at Bocas was not to be trusted. Like George Price, her favourite novelist was Thomas Mann, and we talked of Mann all through an excellent meal of turtle meat.

I returned to the hotel at 10.30 alone. Chuchu wanted to go and look for the 'riotous evening' at the fair. After I had turned out the light in the bathroom and felt my way to the bed, gnawing rat noises began, and cats outside made very vocal love. I wondered how long it would take for the rat to bite through the wooden wall. Chuchu returned, disappointed by the fair – there had been no sign of a 'riotous evening'. As soon as the bathroom light was out the cats again made love and the rat started again to gnaw.

I had a bad night, but I woke with a sense of exhilaration. I thought, wrongly as it proved, that my writer's block was over. The novel was moving through my head. Now that I had decided that it should be laid in an imaginary country and not in Panama, the characters, I felt, might be able to detach themselves from their originals. Chuchu would no longer be Chuchu and Omar would cease to be Omar. Bocas would be there at the end of the road and Chuchu suggested a very suitable name for the place – Cuno del Toro. Chuchu would not be blown up in his car – he would simply disappear for ever in search of his hated dog and Fish Face would be sent by the General to bring the girl back.

I dressed in a state of unreal happiness to find the sun shining and Bocas very nearly transformed. The rain had somehow drained away and the little houses on stilts with their balconies reminded me of Freetown in Sierra Leone, a town I had loved. The military plane arrived punctually at 9.15 to fetch us, and

156

instead of the two and a half hours our journey to Bocas had taken, we returned in an hour and a quarter. The sky was cloudless and we could see dozens of islands scattered below us like a jig-saw puzzle: it was possible to see how each piece had once fitted into another. We gave Raúl a lift, for he hoped to find some support for his campaign in Panama City.

7

After lunch Silvana met us with the news that the beastly dog had returned home. Chuchu and I went to see Omar. He was very cheerful and relaxed, and when he heard of Raúl's sad plight, he at once told Chuchu to give him a thousand dollars for his expenses – 'But say it's a gift from Graham. It wouldn't do for my party to know that I am helping an opponent to fight us.' (In fact I learnt a year later that Raúl by splitting the vote had helped the Communists to win in Bocas against Omar's candidate.)

Omar asked me questions about my writing, how characters evolved. I told him that the hopeful moment in writing a novel was when a character took possession of the writer, spoke words that the writer had not anticipated and behaved in an unpredicted way.

We spoke too of Russia and of a favourite theory of mine that one day the KGB would be in control and it would prove more easy to deal with pragmatists than ideologists. The KGB re-cruited the brightest students from the universities, they learnt foreign languages, they saw the outer world, Marx meant little to them. They could be instruments of a measure of reform at home.

Omar told me, 'What you say interests me. I was visited not long ago by a KGB officer from South America, a young man, very cultivated. He spoke excellent Spanish. I was very cau-tious with him, for I feared a trap. He told me that there could be no change in Russia as long as the old men in the Kremlin were still alive. He said that he would be coming to see me again.'

Did he come? He must have known of Omar's friendship with Carter. Was he planning to pass some signal to Carter through the General before the American elections which Reagan was to win? I shall never know the answer to those questions.

As for the elections, Omar remarked, 'Of course I want Carter to win, but if Reagan wins it may be more fun.' He was still hoping against hope for a confrontation.

Chuchu came to me next morning and told me he had a message from the General. Omar wanted me to go down at once to his house at Farallón. 'He says he's going to treat you as if he was one of your characters and take charge of you.'

We drove down and found a large party going on, with wives and children, and so we made an excuse for not staying to lunch, and after a while the General led the way to a quiet room and there he repeated what he had said to Chuchu. 'I am one of your characters now, Graham, and I am going to take you in charge.'

Joint manoeuvres, he told me, had begun between the American and Panamanian forces. Five hundred American troops had been parachuted into their base in what had been the Canal Zone, and five hundred of the National Guard (probably our old friends the Wild Pigs) had been dropped on Fort Bragg in North Carolina. It was his intention to fly to Fort Bragg on 1 September in order to see how his men were getting on. Well, as one of my characters, he intended to take me under his control. I was to come with him as a Panamanian officer in National Guard uniform ('We'll give you the rank of captain or major or what you like').

It was for a moment a very tempting proposal. I had been a Panamanian delegate with a Panamanian diplomatic passport in Washington. Now to play the part of a Panamanian officer at Fort Bragg . . . it was at least an amusing idea . . . I said, 'But I'm booked to leave for France on 1 September.'

'Stay a few days longer.'

'I'm worried about what's happening there.'

Chuchu had already told him about my problem with the undesirable character in Nice, who had been married to my friend's daughter and now threatened her with the *milieu*. Omar spoke sharply, 'I won't have a friend of mine worried in this way. I'll send a man to France to teach a lesson to this fellow who's troubling you.'

'No. I don't think that's wise.'

'Well, send the young woman over here with her children.'

I spoke of her work which she would have to abandon.

'We'll give her work here.'

'She would be very lonely. She would miss her parents.'

'Then we'd send her back to France with a new name and a Panamanian passport.'

He could see that I was not convinced, and he added, 'It would be much simpler to deal with the man who is threatening her. Are fruit machines legal in France?'

'No, I don't think so. In Monte Carlo . . .'

'There's a certain American here whom I have helped. Go and see him with one of my G-2 officers. I am sure he could arrange to have the man dealt with. He owes me a debt of gratitude.'

I pretended that I would think the matter over.

'Now for Fort Bragg.'

'It wouldn't work, Omar. You would be messing with the American general. I would be in the junior officers' mess. What would they think of an old Panamanian captain with practically no Spanish who spoke English with an English accent?'

I am sorry to this day that at the last meeting we ever had together I disappointed him – not only over Fort Bragg but over the violent solution to all my problems. I have never lost as good a friend as Omar Torrijos.

Time was running out rapidly – rum punches at Montego Bay, dinner at their flat with Chuchu and Silvana and the hateful dog, who resented my presence as though he knew he had become a character in my novel, a last meal at the Peruvian

159

restaurant with Chuchu and Flor, the rum punch girl, whom we had at last tracked down. Luck was with me. At the airport I won enough at the fruit machines to pay for a bottle of duty-free whisky and two cartons of cigarettes.

There was no sadness this time when I caught the plane, for I knew that I would be returning the next year. The telephone in Antibes would ring and Chuchu's voice would come on the line telling me that my ticket awaited me at KLM. I would choose a date in August during the judicial holidays when nothing much could happen over our private war, I would drink again in the Van Gogh lounge in Amsterdam and I would arrive at 9.30 in the morning. Chuchu would be there to meet me and I could already hear him telling me, 'The General wants us down at Farallón for lunch. We'll go in my little plane.' Or perhaps – to my satisfaction, for I was a little uneasy in his plane: 'I have my car here.'

EPILOGUE

1983

1

I found myself sitting in a small military helicopter flying over the mountains and jungle of Panama. Beside me was Omar's daughter Carmen, and her eyes reminded me of her father's; they were honest and give-away. Chuchu of course was with us. The pilot pointed out the area of forest between two mountains where Omar and his companions had crashed to their death. The weather was almost bad enough to have pleased Omar; we bucketed up and down and to and fro in the rain squalls. I think all three of us had in our minds how strange it would be if we came to the same end in the same place where the man we loved had died.

I had not wished to return to Panama. Panama without the presence of Omar Torrijos would, I felt sure, seem a country painfully barren. It was January 1983 and I had come to Panama first in 1976, nearly seven years before. When I had heard of Omar's death in August 1981, it was as though a whole section of my life had been cut out. It was better, I thought, not to revive memories. Chuchu had been frequently on the telephone from Panama trying to persuade me to return. My ticket, which I had failed to use in 1981, he told me, was still there waiting for me in Amsterdam, the President was anxious for me to come, Omar's family wanted me to come, and I could be 'of use'. He never explained what use . . . and I stubbornly said 'no'. I had a good enough reason. My war with the character in Nice still dragged on, and there were three legal proceedings pending against me in France.

'The Nicaraguans want to see you again,' Chuchu's voice said. That I didn't in the least believe, so 'no', I said again and again, 'no', and I can't remember now what it was that at last forced me reluctantly to say 'yes'.

'All right,' I said. 'For two weeks only. I can't leave France for longer.'

2

As the KLM plane from Amsterdam turned away from the Atlantic and began to pass over the great Darién jungle towards the Pacific, I felt a great depression which I tried to diminish first with two glasses of champagne and then with a Bols gin. They didn't raise my spirits.

The name Omar Torrijos stood out over the new international airport and I was more sad than happy to see him commemorated in the great dead letters. Chuchu of course was there to welcome me. He drove me to a huge luxury hotel which was new since my last visit.

'Couldn't we go to the Continental? I always liked the Continental.'

'This is easier for parking my car.'

My heart sank as we were shown into the presidential suite on the fourteenth (really the thirteenth) floor: a sitting-room and bar larger than my whole flat in Antibes, with a bedroom almost as big and three doors to the passage.

'Did you see the fellow I spoke to in the hall?' Chuchu asked me.

'Yes.'

'He's your armed bodyguard. Colonel Diaz, the head of security, has put him on twenty-four-hour duty to look after you.'

I felt less than ever at home. When Omar was alive I had never been so luxuriously lodged nor had I ever been in the care of a G-2 guard – Chuchu and his revolver had been enough, and as Chuchu had remarked to me in the motel at Santiago so many years before, 'A revolver is no defence.'

After more than twelve months of separation we talked and talked and talked, first in the presidential suite, which seemed a little less overpowering after a couple of whiskies, and afterwards at the Basque refugee's restaurant, the Marisco – this at least had not changed, and the security guard who accompanied us everywhere proved to be a pleasant companion.

Chuchu was convinced that Omar had been murdered, that there had been a bomb in the plane, and he spoke of mysterious events which had preceded his death, but he gave as an example two articles which had been published containing attacks on Omar by President Reagan, and it seemed flimsy evidence. I was not convinced. Omar, who had been on good terms with Carter, was a very useful intermediary for the Americans in spite of his social democracy – surely the only people who might have desired his death were the military in El Salvador and perhaps some conservatives at home. But there was certainly one mystery, which I learnt later from his friend Rory González (who told me also that he disbelieved in the bomb): the last four nights before Omar was killed he had spent with his wife. It was as though he had felt some sort of premonition of his end, and wanted to show his kindness and his consistent loyalty to the past which went so much deeper than his infidelities.

As I talked with Chuchu and later with the President, with Rory González, with Colonel Diaz, I began to realize how in a strange fashion, Omar Torrijos was still very much alive in Panama. Chuchu told me that since his death he had dreamt of him every night, and young Ricardo de la Espriella, the President, whom I had met and liked two years before when he was Vice-President, spoke too of his dreams of Omar. ('At his death,' he told me, 'I lost a father and a brother.') His dreams all took more or less the same form – there would be a serious disaster with which as President he felt unable to cope and at the moment of his deepest despair Omar would arrive on the scene. In one dream two trains had crashed head on. There were a great many casualties and the President was at his wits' end what to do when Omar appeared and told him, 'Don't worry. You can manage all right,' and then added as he walked away, 'I am going off to rest.' The President told me that one night he was woken by someone coming into the bedroom, and his wife whispered to him, 'There's someone in the room.' She too had heard the movements, but she did not see the image as he did, of Omar sprawling with one leg crossed easily over the arm of a chair.

Certainly in Panama I found little of the sense of emptiness which I had feared, and yet there were real problems which Chuchu described to me on that first morning, and perhaps the biggest of all was the attitude of the new head of the National Guard, General Paredes. Paredes, who had quickly taken over from the gum-chewing Flores whom I had so mistrusted, was a man of the Right. Apparently he was a friend of General Nutting, the head of the American base in what had been the Canal Zone, he intended to stand for the Presidency in 1984, and he was no friend of the Sandinistas in Nicaragua. The Torrijos dream of a social democratic Central America, independent of the United States but representing no menace to justify intervention, was unlikely to be achieved with the help of General Paredes. Yet another dream too had faded. Work on the great copper mine had ceased – at any rate for the time being.

That first evening Chuchu and I spent with Colonel Diaz, the chief of security, talking until dinner at ten and afterwards till midnight: a man gentle and modest in manner, but I thought I detected in him a disguised firmness and a strong determination to follow the road laid down by Omar. He was more moderate in his assessment of Paredes than Chuchu. It was true, he said, that Paredes had moved towards the right, but he believed that his strain of African blood had not made it easy for him to get on with the conservative oligarchy of the rich and a change of course was still possible.

Diaz was finding his own position difficult. With the signing of the Canal Treaty and the death of Omar the heroic days seemed over for little Panama; there was no one now who could talk like an equal with the world leaders as Omar had talked to Tito, Fidel Castro, Carter, the Pope, and all the heads of state on his tour of Western Europe in 1977 after the signing of the Canal Treaty.* We spoke too of El Salvador: Diaz had little belief in a guerrilla victory, only in a stagnation which might possibly prove to be more valuable than a victory.

Colonel Diaz told me of the four hours which he had recently passed with Fidel Castro. 'I liked him,' he said, 'but I was surprised by one claim which he made, that he had intervened in Angola without the consent of Russia.'

'That doesn't surprise me,' I told Colonel Diaz. As I had always seen it, Castro had embarked first on a revolutionary adventure in South America against the wishes of the USSR, who at that period had no desire for trouble in Latin America, with the result that Che Guevara was betrayed to his death by the Communist Party in Bolivia. I believed, and I believe still, that the Angolan adventure was an attempt by Castro to demonstrate a measure of independence, and it was only when his action proved to be at least partially successful that the USSR came to his support. He had another motive too: there is a very large black population in Cuba and to aid a black government in Africa was a way of separating himself spectacularly from the racialist Cuba of Batista where intermarriage was forbidden and even the bars in Havana were closed to blacks by calling them clubs to which only white men were welcome. There is an odd irony about the situation in Angola. The United States complains of the presence of Cuban troops, but it is the Cuban troops who protect the Gulf Oil installations from being overrun in the civil war with Unita.

Diaz had three plans for me. He wanted me to return to Nicaragua, where the Sandinista leaders knew of my friendship for Omar, as a signal to them that the Torrijos spirit was still alive in Panama. Afterwards I was to visit Cuba and see Fidel

* Chuchu was with him when he saw the Pope, and he introduced Chuchu as 'my Minister of Defence'.

Castro for the same purpose. (The Cuban Ambassador in Panama, he said, would be inviting me.) The third plan was for me to visit the jungle village, known as Ciudad Romero, which had been built by refugees from El Salvador, who had been rescued from their perilous exile in Honduras by Omar. Chuchu at once volunteered to take me to all three places in his little second-hand plane and I hadn't the courage to say no, so I was glad when Diaz said that I must have an army jet to take me to Nicaragua, so as to give my visit an official tone, and as for the village, only a helicopter could reach it.

3

But it was Chuchu who made me feel more than anyone else that the Torrijos spirit was still very much alive. One morning he seemed to be spending an unusually long time in the garage where he bought his petrol. When he returned I asked him what he had been doing. 'Taking photographs,' he said.

'Photographs?'

'Yes. Eden Pastora has bought a boat in Panama. I was able to photograph it where it lay from inside the garage. I want to take the photograph to Nicaragua.'

Another evening after dinner he wanted to go to someone's house. 'I've got something to give him.'

'What?'

'There are two machine-guns in the back of the car.'

'Why does he want a machine-gun?'

'It's not that *he* wants a machine-gun. It's *I* that want a thousand rounds of small-arms ammunition. We are doing a swap.'

'For the Sandinistas?'

'No, no, they have all they want. For El Salvador.'

I was overjoyed at this glimpse of Professor José de Jesús Martínez, poet and mathematician, at his proper job.

4

Next day, I met for the first time the Foreign Office official, Señor Blandón, in charge of organizing what was later to be known as the Contadora group – the diplomatic offensive which it was hoped would prevent war in Central America. The group still works for peace, but the plan was more ambitious in those days. For in addition to Panama, Colombia, Venezuela and Mexico it was even hoped to include Cuba and the United States in the group. Did he really believe, I asked Señor Blandón, that Reagan would agree to join any organization which included Cuba? Yes, he said, with the American elections approaching it was possible that Reagan might feel it desirable politically to join them. He hadn't the support of Congress in his covert operations, and as for open war between Honduras and Nicaragua he must know that there was some unrest among the junior officers in the Honduran army; the El Salvador guerrillas too were strong enough to make a diversion on the borders of Honduras: and the air and tank superiority of Honduras had small importance in the kind of terrain where they would have to fight. It was true that the diplomatic plan was not liked by General Paredes, but it had been approved by the President and the Cubans would be arriving next day to discuss it. He repeated that Fidel Castro had invited me to go to Havana, so it was important for me to see the Cuban Ambassador.

When I visited the Ambassador I had not believed in Castro's invitation, which turned out, as I had thought likely, to be an invitation from the Casa de las Américas to some sort of cultural jamboree in Havana. I told the Ambassador that I was only interested in the political situation. I hadn't time on this visit for culture.

The President later talked to me of my Nicaraguan visit – which seemed to resemble more and more a mission. The message he wanted to convey to the Junta was: don't talk aggressively, but appeal to the Security Council for a United

Nations force on the Honduran border. Panama, a member of the Council, would support such an appeal and if the United States should use her veto Nicaragua would gain a propaganda victory. It seemed a reasonable idea.

After seeing the President I had drinks with Colonel Noriega, the Chief of Staff. He too was keen on my visit to Nicaragua. It was obvious that the right-wing slant of General Paredes embarrassed him as much as the President, and he was disappointed when I told him of my reception at the Cuban Embassy. He said he would take the matter up with the Ambassador. He was sure the invitation had not been a cultural one.

Before leaving for Nicaragua there was for me a rather embarrassing party at the Presidencia at which I received from the President the Grand Cross of the Order of Vasco Núñez de Balboa. (Keats, it will be remembered, in his famous sonnet had confused Balboa with Cortés, who had never gazed at the Pacific with a wild surmise, silent, upon a peak in Darién.) I had done nothing to justify such a decoration, and my sense of embarrassment increased when I became tangled up in the ribbon and the stars. I felt like a Christmas tree in process of being hung with presents. My only merit was that I had been a friend of Omar Torrijos and I could well imagine how he would have laughed at my situation, as I struggled with the ribbon and tried to get the stars into place. All the same there may have been a tactical reason behind the ceremony; the President was perhaps signalling to the Sandinista leaders that they could trust me as a messenger. Whatever the reason and whatever my embarrassment, in the end I had a certain sense of happiness because the kindly gift made one feel a little closer to the country which had produced Omar Torrijos.

There were many in the United States, I was sure, who would consider that I was being 'used', but that thought didn't worry me in the least. They could say that I had been 'used' too in Cuba in 1958 when I carried warm clothes to Santiago for Castro's men in the Sierra Maestra and, through an Irish MP, a friend of mine, I had been able to question the Conservative government in the House of Commons on the sale of old jet planes to Batista, but I regretted nothing then and I regretted nothing now. I have never hesitated to be 'used' in a cause I believed in, even if my choice might be only for a lesser evil. We can never foresee the future with any accuracy.

There was a rather Panamanian comedy about my departure to Managua. Chuchu was with me, of course, and at the airport we learnt that the Nicaraguans had sent a small jet to fetch me, carrying my future host, Mario Castillo, who worked for Humberto Ortega, the Minister of Defence, but the Panamanians were insisting that I should fly in a Panamanian plane. After a lengthy discussion Castillo consented to join us in our plane and the Nicaraguan plane flew alongside of us empty. We drank Señor Castillo's vodka all the way to Managua and that eased any awkwardness in the situation.

5

At Managua I found some familiar faces on the tarmac to welcome me. Father Cardenal, the Minister of Culture, was there and Daniel Ortega's beautiful wife, Rosario, whom I had seen last in San José, Costa Rica, when we drank together out of earshot while Chuchu had his rendezvous with the leader of the Junta. It was the beginning of some very crowded days.

My siesta at the house of Castillo was broken that afternoon by the visit of an old monsignor whom I had been recommended to meet before I left Europe by an Irish professor who had spent some months in Nicaragua. With him I was able to discuss the strange attitude of Archbishop Obando.

The Archbishop had played a very courageous part at the beginning of the civil war. He had in a sense legitimized the war in the eyes of Catholics by publishing a pastoral letter against Somoza which could easily have cost the Archbishop his life. When the National Palace was captured by Eden Pastora he had flown to Panama with Pastora and the men whom Somoza had released, including Tomás Borge, in order to ensure their safety, and now he had turned against the Junta as Pastora had done. Was it only because there were Marxists in the government? I remembered Chile and how Allende had Communist ministers in his government and yet he had never lost the support of the Archbishop of Santiago. Indeed, on the National Day in 1972 I had watched the Archbishop presiding at an ecumenical service in the cathedral attended by all the members of the government, including the Communists. The gospel was read by a Protestant, prayers were said by a Jewish rabbi and the sermon was preached by a Jesuit. Even the Chinese embassy sent their representatives.

The old monsignor had his own theory to account for the Archbishop's change of side. He believed it was wounded vanity. The Archbishop had been in the habit of appearing on television every Sunday saying the Mass in Managua. The new government had decided with reason that the television Mass should be said in a different parish each Sunday – in the cities of Granada and León and also in the country parishes. The Archbishop refused to lose his monopoly, so that the government cancelled the televised Mass altogether.

The government had done their best to reward the Archbishop for the brave stand he had taken at the beginning of the civil war. They had offered to help rebuild the cathedral shattered by the earthquake. He had refused their aid on insufficient grounds. They had offered a large building site for a new cathedral, but he had rejected this because a military camp was to be made nearby. Are soldiers forbidden by the Church to hear Mass?

'He's very conservative,' the old monsignor remarked gently. (As a parish priest he had at great risk sheltered in his home Sandinista refugees from Somoza.) 'He always wears a soutane.' It was as though for Archbishop Obando John XXIII had never lived and Vatican II had never taken place.

Next morning I visited the Centre for Ecumenical Studies.

172

Apart from one American Presbyterian minister, the young government representative at the Vatican and a translator, they were all Catholic priests and they were even more severe critics of the Archbishop than the monsignor. There was, for example, the strange story of the 'sweating Virgin' at Cuapa.

In 1981 the Archbishop inaugurated a Marian campaign, consecrating the country on 28 November to the 'Immaculate Heart of Mary', a rather unnecessary campaign, it might be thought, to wage in Nicaragua which was quite as Catholic a country as Poland. The campaign was promoted by *La Prensa*, the conservative opposition paper, and there was a distinct smell of politics about it.

In December *La Prensa* reported on the 'miracle of the Virgin that perspires'. A wooden image in the church at Cuapa was seen to be sweating and soon pious Catholics were gathering at the improvised altar built for the statuette to collect the sweat with cotton wool. Later the sweat became known as tears (sweat was regarded perhaps as undignified), tears wept for poor Nicaragua under the rule of the Sandinistas. It was strange that she had never wept for Nicaragua under the rule of Somoza.

Usually the Church is very suspicious of miracles and any 'miracle' undergoes strict investigation. No such investigation was made. The Archbishop visited the statuette and his conservative henchman Bishop Vivas announced that there was no human explanation for the perspiration (or the tears).

However, the human explanation was soon found. Each night the statuette had been submerged in water and then put in a deep freeze, so that quite naturally it sweated during the day. The discovery of the fraud, however, received no publicity from *La Prensa* or from the two bishops. Indeed, at the end of 1982 the bishops were planning to make Cuapa an official shrine.

The Pope's forthcoming visit to Central America was discussed at the Centre. Everyone was apprehensive, as it later proved with reason. A new cardinal from South America had

173

been recently appointed, an archbishop who belonged politically to the extreme right, and the right in Latin America is not like the conservative right in Europe. It is the right of the killer gangs in El Salvador and the murderers of Archbishop Romero. Perhaps under the new cardinal's influence, the Pope had made the retirement of the two priests in the government, Father D'Escoto, the Foreign Minister, and Father Cardenal, the Minister of Culture, a condition for his visit. Everyone at the Centre was in favour of refusing the condition. However, it was later withdrawn, but Father D'Escoto went on a very diplomatic mission to India during the papal visit, and television sets all over the world showed white-haired old Cardenal, a very respected poet in Central America, on his knees in front of the Pope, trying to kiss his hand which the Pope snatched from his reach and then wagged a finger in rebuke – an ugly spectacle, which didn't please the crowd, nor were they pleased that the Pope made no reference to the funeral on the same spot the day before of seventeen young Sandinistas murdered by the Contras.

After seeing the priests at the Centre I drove on to a town renamed Ciudad Sandino to visit two American nuns who belonged, like Father D'Escoto, to the Mary Knoll order. The town consisted of about 60,000 very poor inhabitants. The nuns lived in the same conditions as the poor – a tin-roofed hut and a standing pipe for water in the yard. One of the two, quite a young woman, particularly impressed me. She had lived for ten years in the town so that she had experienced the dictatorship of Somoza and the whole civil war.

She spoke of the changes which had been made by the Sandinistas. Under Somoza there had been only one doctor in the town, a lazy and inefficient man. Now there were three clinics, midwives were being trained, and there was a vast improvement in the children's health. Under Somoza no inhabitant had a title to his hut and patch of ground. The whole town was owned by Somozistas who could turn anyone out at will, so that there was no point in planting. Now I could see for my-

174

self how the inhabitants were growing vegetables and even flowers.

I asked about the Miskito Indians. A great deal of anti-Sandinista propaganda had been made about the removal of the Miskitos from where they lived on the Atlantic coastline. This had become the main war zone which was constantly penetrated from Honduras by the Contras led by members of the old Somoza National Guard. Tomás Borge, the Minister of the Interior, himself admitted to me that the Sandinistas had behaved clumsily. They had not explained properly to the Indians, he said, the reason for removing them into camps outside the zone. However, the American nun had visited the camps and she denied the truth of their ill-treatment. She found them well housed and well fed and better cared for medically than they had ever been before.

Next day we started early, at 6.45, for another war zone on the northern frontier with Honduras. We were a party of six, Chuchu and I, a fat bearded doctor, a Cuban journalist, a woman photographer, and our leader, an army captain. When we entered the war zone after Chinandega we were joined by an escort car. A bridge on the main road had been blown up by the Contras and was under repair with the help of Cuban engineers.

We stopped at Somotillo, where there was a military headquarters, and watched the training of the local *milice* – a kind of home guard of peasants and artisans. As it was a Sunday there were many small children watching with their mothers, and I had a feeling of unease when I saw a child of eight posing with a rifle for a photographer – an irrational feeling, for what is the difference to a child between a real rifle and a toy one? A boy of fourteen ran, flung himself to the ground, opened fire at a target beside an old man who looked in his late seventies. I had noticed that in Nicaragua the peasants age early, but when I learned that he had fought years back with Sandino against Somoza and the United States Marines I realized that his looks did not belie his age, for Sandino was killed in 1934. He had

175

great dignity and spoke to me very seriously, when he heard that I was a writer, of García Márquez. When I said that 'Gabo' was a friend of mine he shook my hand.

As we drove on along the frontier the road was almost empty of traffic and it was dominated all its length by the hills on the Honduran side. According to our leader, two or three deaths were caused almost daily by indiscriminate mortar fire from Honduras to which there was no way of replying if Nicaragua were not to be accused of making war on Honduras. None the less I suspect it was a fairly peaceful section of the war zone to which they were taking us. Finally we reached a small town, Santo Tomás, which was three kilometres from the frontier – indeed one end of the town, where the *milice* had their head-quarters (an old *milice* lay asleep on the floor with his rifle for a pillow), was only three hundred yards from Honduras. Trenches had been dug in a semi-circle against a possible attack and for our benefit an exercise was held. An alarm was sounded and the *milice* took to the trenches – old men and boys leaping down and taking up positions with varying agility. The spirit was there – but not always the physical ability. It was a spectacle which would have amused and delighted Omar. All through those days I missed his presence and spoke of him often – to Tomás Borge, to Daniel Ortega, the head of the Junta, to Humberto Ortega, the Minister of Defence and head of the army, to Lenin Cerna, the head of security, to Father Cardenal to whom he had given refuge in Panama. Sometimes I found myself wondering whether Eden Pastora would have deserted his companions if Omar had lived.

Next day, when I visited Tomás Borge at his home and met his wife and child, I found my mission was not quite so easy as I had thought. He proved to be critical of both Colonel Diaz and Colonel Noriega. Perhaps they seemed a little tainted in his eyes by the fact that their official leader was General Paredes.

I suppose for a man like Borge, who has been imprisoned, fought and suffered in a civil war, there must often be an impatience with patience. Omar had shared that impatience, even though he reluctantly controlled his own. But in Panama now bloodshed seemed a long way off: it was not the natural form for a revolution to take there. General Paredes, the friend of the American General Nutting, would not be at the head of the National Guard for much longer: he had got to resign in order to stand for the presidency in 1984 – indeed, he was to resign the next year before the election date. As Díaz had said, the heroic days in Panama were over – the days when Omar was ready, if he failed to get his Treaty, to sabotage the Canal and take to the mountains and jungle, while in Nicaragua the heroic days continued, the fight against Somoza had been succeeded by the confrontation with the Contras, with Pastora, with Honduras and behind them with the immense power of the United States. Perhaps to Borge Panama without Omar was only the Panama of 163 banks and the rich foreigners' yachts sailing under the Panama flag and the oligarchy of which I had not yet had a glimpse: confrontation with the United States belonged, apart from Omar and the Wild Pigs, only to the students, to the slums of the cities, to the *barrios* of the poor like El Chorillo. To many of the peasants in the countryside politics, as I had witnessed, meant very little beyond the price of yucca, while in Nicaragua almost the whole country has risen against the tyrant and the armed forces.

Borge took me to see Lenin Cerna, the head of security, who showed me his small museum dedicated to proofs of American intervention: military clothes bearing the American manufacturers' name and address, and some very unpleasant explosives disguised as EverReady torches and, even worse, one made up as a Mickey Mouse picnic box (marked 'Walt Disney Productions'), magnetized so that it could be stuck on the side of a car – an irresistible attraction to any child. The head of American intelligence had been visiting Nicaragua, and when I lunched with Humberto Ortego and his staff I asked him if he had shown the general these bombs. 'Yes,' Ortega replied, 'and he told me that they didn't come from the army.' He said that the general had begun their conversation with a hint of blackmail, but he had ended in a more friendly spirit by admitting that there were some differences between the Pentagon and the State Department. I remembered how the Pentagon had warned Carter that 100,000 troops would be needed to guard the Canal and the Zone. How many would be needed to take over Nicaragua?

6

On my last night in Nicaragua I received an unexpected visit which has left a sad memory behind it. Chuchu and I were still the guests of Señor Castillo, who was assisting the business side of the Ministry of Defence, in a beautiful house and garden with a beautiful hostess, guarded by uniformed sentries, where I felt, I must admit, a little isolated from the Sandinista revolution. I had a room in the house and Chuchu occupied a small guest house in the garden. Then a message came to us that Marcial wanted to visit me, but he didn't wish to come to the main house. A rendezvous was made for a meeting in the guest house.

I had not met Salvador Cayetano since we had spoken together in Panama in 1981, when I made a vain appeal for the life of the South African Ambassador. His code name Marcial seemed now an unnecessary precaution, for I noticed that though he used it in a *dédicace* which he wrote for me that night, the book which he inscribed had been published under his proper name. Perhaps two years before that would have seemed a lapse in security. Cayetano was one of the commanders of the combined guerrilla forces of the FMLN in El Salvador and he may not have fully trusted the atmosphere of bourgeois comfort in the home of Ortega's business associate, so that he had no wish to pass through the house. He arrived with two of his own armed bodyguards at the guest house in the garden.

Time had published an unfortunate note on our previous

meeting. I had rashly commented to my friend Diederich that Cayetano had the most merciless eyes I could remember seeing and that I wouldn't like to have been his prisoner. The remark had been taken out of the context where I had spoken of Cayetano's own sufferings from prison and torture, and though *Time* had published my letter of correction, their first note was taken up and used against him by the right-wing press in El Salvador. I had expected therefore a certain chill at our second meeting. Nothing of the sort happened. He brushed aside my apologetic reference – the affair had no importance – and he greeted me with what seemed almost affection. Since I had seen him last he had grown a little wisp of a Ho Chi Minh beard and looked much older than his age, sixty-three. And I would no longer have described his eyes as merciless.

He got down at once to business, spreading a large map of El Salvador over his knees. With his tiny fingers he rapidly pointed out the military and guerrilla positions and the strategy which he intended to follow – an attack here, an attack there, a shift of guerrillas from that area to this. He seemed reasonably confident of success. Perhaps if I had been a secret agent this might have been valuable information or disinformation. The fate which overtook him three months later makes me wonder whether he was in the habit of giving his trust too easily.

After he had finished and folded up his map we talked in more general terms. I asked him what he did about his prisoners, who must be an encumbrance to guerrillas, and I recalled how in the Sierra Maestra during the Cuban civil war Castro had taken away his prisoners' trousers and set them loose. 'It's boots not trousers that we need,' Cayetano said. 'We take their boots and let them go. We have a terrible need of boots. In the kind of country where we are fighting a pair of boots will only last about a month,' and I remembered Omar's dream of finding himself without boots in the jungle. Cayetano added that arms were not a serious problem. Arms could be bought anywhere and anyway a regular supply was captured from the enemy.

179

I asked him about the future if they won their war. He claimed that there would be complete religious freedom in El Salvador. I only report what he said, and of course he knew that he was talking to a Roman Catholic. The future alone will show whether he spoke the truth, but it is common knowledge that Archbishop Damas is taking the same heroic stand in El Salvador against the death squads as Archbishop Romero, and Cayetano told me that the guerrillas had received much help from individual priests. I believe he spoke sincerely, and perhaps he was beginning to distance himself from the bitterness of his past suffering. He had no belief – that was obvious – in a political solution.

Before he left he gave me a copy of his only book, *Secuestro y Capucha* ('Kidnapped and Hooded'), inscribed to his '*Querido Hermano*', embraced me with a certain tenderness and disappeared into the garden with his two guards. Three months later he killed himself.

Cayetano was in Libya (arranging the delivery of arms with Gaddafi? Who knows?) when news reached him that his deputy and close comrade for many years, Comandante Mélida Anaya, had been brutally murdered in Managua. Political reasons for murder are not uncommon, but one can see no reason for the savagery with which this murder was committed. Eighty stab wounds were found in her body and as a *coup de grâce* the murderers had cut her throat. When Cayetano got back to Managua the two men who had committed the murder were under arrest and so was the man who had ordered the deed. The ringleader, so it was reported, was the man in the guerrilla group whom he most trusted. Cayetano shot himself through the heart, sitting in an armchair. How can we in the West judge such a man or measure his suffering?

The three men are still in prison in Managua waiting the time, if it ever comes, when they can be handed over for trial to a popular government in El Salvador, and since Cayetano's death the mystery of the murder and the suicide has deepened yet further. It is said that Mélida Anaya had grown to be in favour of a political solution to the war. Cayetano's own FPL group had thus become divided, and it was even suggested that Cayetano had ordered her death. But why the brutality? If guilty, why did he return to Managua? Will we ever know the truth?

7

Next day I started on the last stage of the programme which had been arranged for me. Humberto and Daniel Ortega had checked with Cuba and I was assured that my invitation was from Fidel Castro and not from the Casa de las Américas. The Nicaraguans provided a small jet plane, which I was told had formerly been the personal plane of Somoza, and when I chose my seat, the pilot was amused. 'You have chosen Somoza's,' he said.

Chuchu and I now had a rather odd companion whom Chuchu had somehow picked up in Nicaragua. He had begged Chuchu to give him a lift to Panama. Apparently he was a Colombian guerrilla who after nineteen years in the jungle wanted to return home and take advantage of an amnesty offered by the new president, but as he had no papers he couldn't travel on a commercial plane. Chuchu planned to lodge him in Panama with Rogelio and Lidia, as he had done with the dubious professor from Guatemala, until he could arrange for him to have a passport. (Chuchu was a man of infinite resource when it came to smuggling arms or men, but I felt sorry for poor Rogelio and Lidia.) The Colombian was a man who spoke very little. He wore a cap even at meals, and he trimmed his nails on to the cloth while he ate.

We were met at Havana by an old acquaintance of mine, Otero, who had travelled with me and the poet Pablo Fernández around Cuba in 1966, and by the then head of security, Piñeiro, whom I had last seen the same year playing basketball with Raúl Castro and other ministers at two in the morning watched by their patient wives. His forbidding red beard had turned snow white, which gave him a patriarchal air. While driving to the house on the outskirts of Havana where we were to be lodged for the night, we talked of this and that and I was astonished to learn that the man who had been head of Cuban security for so long still imagined that MI5 and MI6 were rival branches of military intelligence. I thought it was unnecessary – and perhaps a little humiliating for him – to correct his error. We lunched together and then Piñeiro went off to arrange the meeting with Castro.

In the evening we went for our rendezvous to the house where my friend García Márquez was installed. Castro had been dining at the Spanish Embassy with Gabo. I had not seen Castro since we passed some hours of the night together in 1966, and he had given me a painting by my friend Porto Carrero. He seemed younger, thinner and more carefree. I produced a formula in greeting him which amused him, 'I am not a messenger. I am the message.' In other words, I had been flown to Nicaragua by the two colonels, Diaz and Noriega, and afterwards to Cuba by the Ortegas, as the known friend of Omar Torrijos, to indicate that in spite of General Paredes the ideas of Torrijos were still very much alive in Panama.

Castro remarked, 'It would be a good thing if Paredes were elected President, for then he would have little power to harm. It would be unfortunate if the conservatives ran a candidate against him who won. Then there would be a conservative president and the danger of a conservative general.'

As for the war in El Salvador, Castro proved as optimistic as Cayetano. He believed that the guerrillas would reach power by the end of 1983. By this time we know that Colonel Diaz, who believed in a long and inconclusive struggle, came nearer the truth.

Castro had read – probably at Gabo's insistence – about one third of my novel *Monsignor Quixote* and this led us to the subject of wine, in which he proved unexpectedly interested. He had read too about my difficulties with Nice justice.

Gabo then introduced the subject of Russian roulette, which I had played in my adolescence (as usual with Gabo he got the facts wrong, saying that I had played the game in Vietnam). Castro wanted to know exactly the circumstances, the number of times I had played and at what intervals. He told me, 'You shouldn't be alive.'

'That is not true. Mathematically each time one plays the odds are the same – five to one against death. The odds are not affected by the number of times you play.'

'No, no. You are wrong there. The odds are not the same.' He began to make abstruse calculations which I couldn't follow and concluded again, 'You shouldn't be alive.'

He then wanted to know what *régime* I followed.

'No *régime*. I eat what I like and drink what I like.'

This obviously shocked him, for he followed a very strict *régime* himself, and he quickly changed the subject.

As in 1966 it was in the early hours of the morning that we said goodbye. At the door he said with a smile, 'Tell them that I have received the message.'

That night in the bathroom I was very startled. I went to urinate and there was a piece of brown paper in the toilet. When my pee touched it the brown scrap leapt out of the bowl and landed on the wall above my head. It was a frog. Perhaps that will be the most enduring memory of my last visit to Communist Cuba. I never knew before that a frog could jump more than six feet in a vertical take-off.

8

A few hours later I was back in Panama, where I was not at all unhappy to find that I had lost my pretentious suite which had been allotted now to an important visitor, Mr Kissinger. I was less happy that I had lost also a gold coloured tie given to me by someone I loved – perhaps Mr Kissinger inherited that too. My agreeable bodyguard was now protecting Mr Kissinger.

Colonel Diaz called on me and I reported on my trip. He insisted that my knowledge of Panama was incomplete without seeing something of the life of the upper bourgeoisie to whom Omar had been anathema. I must go that evening with him to a house-warming given by an acquaintance of his. 'But please don't tell anyone that you have been in Nicaragua and Cuba.'

The party was a nightmare, and I was without the support of Chuchu. One could hear the noise from two streets away. There was a buffet in the garden, but I was never able to reach it, for it was separated from me by hundreds of guests who were all shouting at the top of their voices in order to make themselves heard above the din of a band which was determined to dominate the guests. One guest bellowed into my ear, 'Just over from England?' And mischievously I ignored the warning of Colonel Diaz.

'No, Cuba.'

'Where?' he asked with incredulity.

'Cuba,' I shouted back, 'and Nicaragua.'

He thrust his way into the crowd to escape and I thrust my way out of it. Would these be the people who elected the next president?

9

So it was that I found myself with Omar's daughter, tossed hither and thither in the helicopter. We were on the way back from visiting the village named in memory of the murdered Archbishop of San Salvador, the first archbishop to be murdered at the altar while celebrating Mass since St Thomas à Becket.

Ciudad Romero had been carved out of the jungle on some low ground beyond the mountain village of Coclesito, where Omar had built himself his modest house and where three years back I had visited the buffaloes. There were four hundred and twenty refugees from El Salvador in the village, and nearly half of them were young children – a few of these had been born in their new home. Their old homes had been destroyed by bombs from the air and then burnt by the military. They had fled to Honduras, where they had found their conditions almost as bad and as perilous as in El Salvador. I don't know in what way Omar got to know of their plight, but he sent a plane to fetch them to Panama. After arrival they were left for a while at a military post at Cimarrón to recuperate and then the village headman was asked to choose a site to build his own village. He chose this site in the jungle because of the fertility of the soil, because of the inexhaustible supply of wood for the houses, and because it was on the banks of a navigable river, so that supplies which would otherwise have had to come by air could come by sea, for there were no roads through the jungle.

All the villagers had congregated in the schoolhouse to welcome us, to welcome in particular Omar's daughter, for the memory of Omar was very dear to them. Whenever he went to his house in Coclesito he would take a helicopter to the village and his pockets were always full of sweets for the children. One of the villagers spoke of the poem he had written in honour of Omar and I asked to hear it. It had been set to music by another of the peasants and he sang his poem accompanied by a drum, a guitar and a violin.

The villagers must have heard the poet sing his poem many times, but they listened with grave intensity. They were hearing the story of their own lives. It was as though they felt it to have become part of literature. The poem was all in eight-syllabled lines and the sound of the half rhymes seemed to transform it into a rough poetry. (Chuchu has translated the words for me.)

Voy a contar una historia:	I am going to tell a story
lo que mi Pueblo sufría	About how my people suffered
por una Junta asesina	On account of a murderous Junta
que compasión no tenía.	That had no compassion.

Cuando un Primero de Mayo
dos aviones bombardearon
y los soldados quemaron
las casitas que teníamos.

One first of May
Two airplanes bombed us
And then the soldiers burned
The little houses we had.

De alli salimos a Honduras,
llegamos a Las Estancias.
allí estuvimos seis meses
bajo mucha vigilancia.

We went then to Honduras
And arrived at Las Estancias
Where they kept us for six months
Under very strict surveillance.

Venimos a Panamá,
nos fuimos pa' Cimarrón
allí estuvimos un tiempo
sólo en recuperación.

Then we came to Panama
And we went to Cimarrón
Where we stayed for some time
To rest awhile.

El Gobierno panameño
fue el que asilo nos dió,
y el señor Omar Torrijos,
General de División.

It was the Panamanian
   Government
And Señor Omar Torrijos,
A General of Division,
That gave us asylum.

Hoy Panamáestá de luto,
lo sentimos su dolor,
porque ha perdido a un gran
   hombre,
hombre de mucho valor.

Today Panama is mourning
And we also feel their pain,
Because they have lost a great
   man,
A man of much courage.

El General fue un lider,
lider de fama mundial,
y que luchó por los pobres,

The General was a leader,
A leader of world fame,
Who fought on behalf of the poor

sincero y muy popular,

A man sincere and very loved.

Este Pueblo panameño
y su Guardia Nacional,
yo los admiro y los quiero,
es un Pueblo fraternal.

I admire and love
The Panamanian people
And their National Guard.
It is a very fraternal people.

Los Latinoamericanos	We Latin Americans
decimos en voz popular:	Say with one voice:
no lo olvidaremos jamás	We shall never forget
al querido General.	Our dear General.
Ya con ésta se despiden	With this we say farewell,
los humildes campesinos	We, the humble peasants
que viven fuera 'e su Patria	That live far away from
por un Gobierno asesino.	their homeland
	Because of a murderous
	government.

One girl among the villagers held my attention because of the melancholy beauty of her eyes. She looked about sixteen and I thought her to be the young mother of the child whom she held between her knees, but when she stood up to go when the song was over I realized that she was only a small child herself, no more than twelve – it was fire, bombs and death which had given her a too-early maturity.

The meeting in the school area over, there was something the peasants urgently wanted to show us. I heard the world 'altar', 'altar', often repeated as they led us to the outskirts of the village, and there sure enough was an altar which they had built and it bore the photograph of the murdered Archbishop in the centre and photographs of Omar at each side. I remembered the abandoned church I had seen in Coclesito with the hens pecking in the aisle and I remembered too what Omar had said about village cemeteries on the first day that we met nearly seven years before: 'If the people don't look after the dead they don't look after the living.' These people without a doubt were looking after their dead.

10

The time had come to say my goodbyes, but first there was an obligation I had to fulfil. General Paredes was certainly not one of those who had tried to keep alive the ideas and ideals of Torrijos, but I could hardly leave Panama without seeing him and thanking him for the plane to Managua and the helicopter to the village of Romero. He invited me to lunch at a new restaurant, named the Charlot in honour of Charlie Chaplin, and I accepted, but then a warning reached me from the owner of the restaurant. One of my fellow guests would be a Cuban refugee journalist who had come from Miami in Kissinger's wake. No journalist in my experience is wholly trustworthy, but a Cuban refugee . . . what a story this man might invent of my visit to Fidel Castro. I sent a message back that I was sorry, but I wouldn't be able to lunch if the journalist were there, and the General altered his guest list. To his credit he showed no resentment at my interference.

It was strange finding myself back for apéritifs in the house which Omar had shared with his friend Rory González and which was now occupied by General Paredes. There were not many obvious changes, but inevitably there was a great sense of emptiness, and I looked around in vain for Omar's budgerigar. No Omar and no budgerigar. Colonel Diaz was there and Colonel Noriega, to whom I was able to pass on an invitation to Nicaragua from Lenin Cerna. To Paredes I gave Fidel Castro's good wishes for the presidential election. Paredes seemed to take these wishes at their face value with a smile of gratification.

Had Castro's good wishes even affected his ideology? I was surprised at lunch to hear him criticize Reagan's policy in Central America and he even had some kind words for the Sandinistas. He seemed anxious to show me that he was following the Torrijos line and in the middle of lunch he presented me with an extravagantly expensive watch inscribed 'To an English brother of General Omar Torrijos from General Paredes'. To refuse the present was impossible, but it was an embarrassing gift. I couldn't help being aware of the cynical amusement of the other guests who knew what my mission had been.

General Paredes did not follow the Torrijos line for very long after the lunch. A few months later I read of how he had paid a visit to Costa Rica where he spoke against the policy of his own President and against the peace-making activities of the Contadora group, and later a certain mystery surrounded him, for a few months after retiring from the National Guard in order to begin his campaign for the presidency it was announced that he had retired from the conflict. Then weeks later the puzzle became more complex. It was reported that he was not standing in the election for the presidency because if he were defeated it would reflect on the National Guard. Had he realized what lay behind Castro's good wishes, and was there now a danger of the result Castro feared? However, I was reassured by Chuchu on the telephone the other day – Paredes, he said, was *kaput*.

That night I gave a farewell dinner in the Peruvian restaurant to my friends, to Chuchu and Silvana, Rogelio and Lidia and, inevitably, the Colombian refugee who had not yet obtained the papers he needed and who still wore a hat and trimmed his nails at the table. Nineteen years of humid jungle life perhaps make the nails grow fast.

Next day, while I waited for my plane in the diplomatic lounge at the airport, Kissinger entered to a barrage of flashlights. I would have liked to ask him whether he had my gold tie, but I wanted to escape quickly, for the Cuban journalist was on the same plane to Miami and he had spotted me. My old bodyguard was drinking coffee by the door, so there was another goodbye to be said. I got the impression that he preferred the more convivial life he had led with me and Chuchu to life in the shadow of Kissinger.

It was a goodbye also to Panama, a little country for which after seven years I had formed a great affection. Five or six times since I began to write this last chapter the telephone has rung and brought me the voice of Chuchu urging me to return. 'The

189

Nicaraguans want you,' he always adds as an inducement, which I take with a big grain of salt. But all the same I find myself unable to give him a firm 'No, no, I can't come again.' Although Panama belongs to the past, to a section of my life which is over, I hedge, I prevaricate. Perhaps in three months, I say . . . or four . . . perhaps next year it will be possible, for to pronounce a final 'no' to Chuchu would be to close finally the pages of a book and relegate to a shelf all the memories which it contains of a dead man whom I loved, Omar Torrijos.

POSTSCRIPT

I have been perhaps unduly sceptical of any part played by the CIA in the death of Omar Torrijos. Since writing this book a document has reached me which is apparently a minority report dated 11 June 1980 addressed to the State Department in Washington.

The writer, or writers, speak of the vital importance of Panama for the United States in connection with El Salvador. 'General Torrijos, who continues to exercise control over the armed forces and veto power over government policies, is described in our character profiles as "volatile, unpredictable . . . a populist demagogue with a visceral anti-American bias . . . and a penchant for the bottle", hardly the description of a reliable ally. Our precarious situation in Panama was recently evidenced by President Royo's public condemnation of our training programme for the Salvadoreans.

'Consider the following additional bonds between Panama and El Salvador:

* Although initially supportive of the 10.15.79 coup, General Torrijos – and the Panamanian Government – have improved ties with the FDR/DRU moderates [on the left].
* Panama's economic difficulties and its dependence on the US banking community make it potentially responsive to our pressure. However, the same factors, combined with our tendency to act heavy-handedly, may encourage a resurgence of "anti-Imperialist" sentiment.
* In the past six months, Panama has been expressing its displeasure on a number of issues related to perceived grievances linked to the implementation of the treaties.

* General Torrijos is in a position to assert control over two key
  tactical resources in any direct US military operations in the
  region: the canal and the bases.'

  Another document issued a month earlier by the Council of
Inter-American Security at 305 4th Street, Washington, speaks
of 'the brutally aggressive extreme Left dictatorship of Omar
Torrijos' and criticizes President Carter's friendly relationship
with Torrijos. Neither of these reports would have affected that
relationship – Carter would have known with what bias and
inaccuracy they had been written, but by the end of the year
Reagan had come to power.

  So it is that I begin to wonder whether the rumour current in
Panama of a bomb concealed in a tape recorder which was
carried unwittingly by a security guard in Omar Torrijos's plane
is to be totally discounted. I cannot but remember the explosive
EverReady torch and Walt Disney picnic box which I saw in
Managua. The plane was a Canadian plane and Canadian
experts examined the wreckage. I would much like to read their
report. I am told that they found no sign of engine trouble
which leaves us with the alternative, a pilot's error or a bomb.